ARISTOTELIAN SOCIETY

Supplementary Volume XXII.

LOGICAL POSITIVISM AND ETHICS

THE SYMPOSIA READ AT THE JOINT SESSION OF
THE ARISTOTELIAN SOCIETY AND THE
MIND ASSOCIATION AT DURHAM,
JULY 9TH—11TH, 1948.

HARRISON AND SONS, LTD.
45, ST. MARTIN'S LANE, LONDON, W.C.2.

1948.

Reprinted with the permission of The Aristotelian Society, London
JOHNSON REPRINT CORPORATION   JOHNSON REPRINT COMPANY LTD.
111 Fifth Avenue, New York, N.Y. 10003   Berkeley Square House, London, W1X6BA

First reprinting, 1969, Johnson Reprint Corporation
Printed in the United States of America

CONTENTS.

PAGE

ADDRESS—ETHICS WITHOUT PROPOSITIONS.
    By WINSTON H. F. BARNES 1

SYMPOSIUM: ARE ALL PHILOSOPHICAL QUESTIONS, QUESTIONS OF LANGUAGE?
    I. By STUART HAMPSHIRE 31
    II. By AUSTIN DUNAN JONES 49
    III. By S. KÖRNER 63

SYMPOSIUM: THE EMOTIVE THEORY OF ETHICS.
    I. By RICHARD ROBINSON 79
    II. By H. J. PATON 107
    III. By R. C. CROSS 127

SYMPOSIUM: WHAT CAN LOGIC DO FOR PHILOSOPHY?
    I. By K. R. POPPER 141
    II. By WILLIAM KNEALE 155
    III. By PROFESSOR A. J. AYER 167

SYMPOSIUM: THINGS AND PERSONS.
    I. By PROFESSOR D. M. MACKINNON 179
    II. By PROFESSOR H. A. HODGES 190
    III. By J. WISDOM 202

THE INAUGURAL ADDRESS.

ETHICS WITHOUT PROPOSITIONS.

By Winston H. F. Barnes.

The epistemological contention that ethical statements do not express propositions[1] or, as I prefer to say, do not assert anything, excites and attracts for three reasons. First, it is thought to be associated with the bold epistemological doctrines of the Logical Positivists. It shares the glamour of their radical speculations. Secondly, it seems to knock the bottom out of our moral convictions (ethical theories based on this contention have in fact been stigmatised as non-moral)[2]; and there is something surprising in the discovery that the foundations of morality can tremble at a whiff of epistemological grape-shot. Thirdly, most of us feel *some* difficulty in deciding whether an ethical statement asserts a peculiar *ethical* fact, or an ordinary sort of fact about the effects of some action, or a fact about people's attitude towards the action. If ethical statements are not assertions at all, we seem to be relieved of this difficulty. We need not choose between the different theories—naturalist or non-naturalist, objectivist or subjectivist. We have been trying to decide what to buy, only to discover that we need puzzle our heads no longer. We have no money.

Owing to these exciting associations, ethical theories taking their start from this contention—which I shall henceforward refer to as the negative contention—have been violently embraced and violently attacked, and sometimes

---

[1] For suggestions of this kind about "good," see A. E. Duncan-Jones as reported by C. D. Broad in " Is ' Goodness ' a Name of a Simple Non-natural Quality ? " *Ar. Soc. Proc.* (1933–4) ; W. H. F. Barnes, " A Suggestion about Values." *Analysis*, March, 1934 ; for the contention applied to " ought " in detail, see A. J. Ayer, *Language, Truth and Logic* (1936), ch. 6 ; R. Carnap, *Philosophy and Logical Syntax* (1935) ; for the detailed exposition of an ethical theory worked out within the limits of the contention, see C. L. Stevenson, *Ethics and Language* (1944).

[2] E. F. Carritt, *Ethical and Political Thinking*, p. 28.

even ridiculed.[3] They deserve, I believe, a more sober examination, because the grounds on which they have been both embraced and attacked are largely irrelevant. As I hope will appear, the contention does not imply any specially positivist doctrine in epistemology. Secondly, it does not imply a non-moral or sceptical theory of conduct. Thirdly, it does not altogether remove our difficulties in choosing between different theories in ethics; rather, it transposes them into another key.

Even if the contention be obviously false, we may by pursuing it discover some features about ethical statements that have passed unnoticed hitherto. But I would not admit for a moment that it is obviously false. Ethical statements are traditionally held to be normative assertions. But how can a statement both assert a fact and prescribe a norm? There seems an obvious difference between telling some one that something is the case and telling him to do something; between deciding that something is so and deciding to do something; between stating that some one is acting in a certain way and recommending approval of his so acting. To deny that ethical statements are normative is to deprive them of their practical rôle; to deny that they are assertions has its difficulties, no doubt, but perhaps the difficulties may be overcome. It would be unwise, however, to minimise them. Suppose I say to a friend *You are late, since you promised to be here by five o'clock and it is now five minutes past five*: and he replies *No, I am not late, since I promised to be here by five past five*. I make an assertion and give my reason for it. He makes a counter-assertion which contradicts mine and gives *his* reason for it. Taken together, the two assertions constitute an argument. Suppose I say to him *You ought to go to the meeting tonight, since you promised the speaker you would* and he replies *I am under no obligation to go since I did not promise but merely expressed an intention*: here also, there seems to be an argument consisting of assertion and counter-

---

[3] Prof. Broad says: "It is the kind of theory which can be swallowed only after one has undergone a long and elaborate process of 'conditioning' which was not available in the eighteenth century." *Ar. Soc. Proc.*, vol. XLV (1944-5), p. 133. He is not distinguishing the various forms the theory may take, but grouping them all together under the title "Interjectional Theory." No doubt there are crude forms of the theory which are merely ridiculous.

assertion, each with its reason. If the negative contention is true the parallelism is not what it seems to be. For in the latter case there are no assertions, no contradiction, and no argument. Any account, to be at all plausible, must find some means of allowing that there are two people saying something to one another and engaged in controversy about some matter. Further, unless we find the writings of moral philosophers completely meaningless, we must be prepared to offer some explanation of what they are doing when they suppose themselves to be discussing the truth or falsity of ethical principles.

In what follows I propose first to clarify the negative contention that ethical statements are not assertions; secondly, to review some positive theories that have been suggested or suggest themselves of what ethical statements in this event might be; and finally to outline the kind of theory which would allow a plausible account to be given of ethical controversy and the writings of moral philosophers.

First, let me try to dispel some misunderstandings that have collected around the negative contention.

(1) Some philosophers holding this view have spoken of ethical statements as pseudo-assertions or pseudo-propositions and have thereby set up an unnecessary resistance to the contention in the minds of their readers. To call them by these names is to suggest, however unintentionally, that they play a deceitful rôle, as when one calls a person a pseudo-intellectual.[4] But if they are not assertions, the fact that most philosophers have taken them to be such, reveals only a mistake on the philosophers' part, and no deceit on the part of the statements. It would have been an odd idea if the man who first discovered that whales had hair and mammary glands, had called them pseudo-fishes because his predecessors had mistakenly thought them to be fishes. They certainly look and behave in some ways like fishes. And ethical statements look and behave in some ways like assertions. But we are quite familiar with this misleading appearance. *Full academic dress will be worn* is a

---

[4] Perhaps *some* of them *have* intended to be disparaging about ethical statements.

statement that looks like an assertion but is unmistakably a command.

(2) Again, though it would be untrue to say that the negative contention has been devised to make ethical statements fit in with a positivist epistemology,[5] those who have maintained it have sometimes held positivist tenets. It is, however, clearly possible to hold that ethical statements are not assertions without holding either (*a*) that assertions and only assertions can be true or false or (*b*) that verifiable, and only verifiable, statements are assertions. A positivist would, I think, hold both (*a*) and (*b*). From (*a*), (*b*) and a third proposition (*c*), that ethical statements are unverifiable, the negative contention follows, as also the further proposition that ethical statements are neither true nor false. To refute (*b*) is to destroy *one* reason that may be given for the negative contention, but not to refute the contention itself. Not positivists only, but most philosophers, would accept (*a*), but as I feel some inclination to think that ethical statements are not assertions and some inclination to think they can be true or false, I must leave it open at this stage. We are, then, to consider the contention that ethical statements are not true or false assertions, without prejudging the question whether what is not an assertion can be true or false in any sense.

(3) There is a further misunderstanding in the notion that, if we hold the negative contention about statements containing the word *obligation*, we subscribe to " the denial that there really is any obligation."[6] This is put in another way when it is said that the theory is non-moral. It is clearly important to refute this charge. But it is difficult to do so as those who bring it offer no proof. It is not difficult to suggest a form of argument which might have led to this conclusion, as follows :—

"(i) The statement *There is an obligation to keep promises* is not a true assertion.

(ii) Therefore it is not a true assertion that there is an obligation to keep promises.

---

[5] As Sir David Ross holds in his *Foundations of Ethics*, p. 35.
[6] Mr. Carritt takes it to involve this denial in his *Ethical and Political Thinking*, p. 28.

ETHICS WITHOUT PROPOSITIONS.

(iii) Therefore there is not an obligation to keep promises.

(iv) What applies to this statement about obligation applies to all statements about obligation.

(v) Therefore there are no obligations to do anything."

This reasoning gives rise to the following paradox, that if we start from the premiss " The statement *There is an obligation to keep promises* is not a false assertion " (which is equally true on the negative contention), we can prove by the same reasoning that there are obligations to do anything whatever. That is, it follows from the contention that any act whatever is both obligatory and not obligatory. There must clearly be a fallacy in the reasoning ; and it is not difficult to see where it lies. We cannot pass from (i) " The statement *There is an obligation to keep promises* is not a true assertion " to (ii) " Therefore it is not a true assertion that there is an obligation to keep promises." It is easy to see that we cannot by considering the following example :—

(i) The statement *I promise to pay* is not a true or false assertion.

(ii) Therefore it is not a true assertion that I promise to pay.

(iii) Therefore I do not promise to pay.

The argument is obviously fallacious, for the statement which is denied to be an assertion by (i) is treated as an assertion in (ii).

(4) There is another misunderstanding ; the notion that on this view ethical statements are meaningless. The contention that they are not assertions in no way implies this. *Be good enough to shut the door* though not an assertion, is clearly meaningful. Perhaps positivists have sometimes spoken as though what is not a verifiable assertion is not meaningful, but I think that all they have wished to say is that it is not a meaningful assertion ; and clearly if it is not an assertion, it is not a meaningful assertion. *Perhaps* some of them have thought that a man could not *say* anything

unless he *asserted* something. If so, they have been confused.[7]

(5) Finally, there is the belief that if ethical statements are not assertions, they must be irrational. This would follow if the sole rational function of language were the making of assertions. But this is a theory which could not commend itself to anyone out of the study.

If ethical statements are not assertions, what are they? The theories I propose to consider may conveniently be called Expressive theories of ethical statements, because they maintain that ethical statements do not make assertions but express something in the mind of the speaker.[8] We may distinguish the traditional theories by calling them Assertive. In what follows I shall limit myself to statements containing the ethical words *ought, obligation, duty, right*, and not try to deal with statements containing the word *good*. I shall consider basic ethical statements such as those beginning with the phrases *You ought, I ought*, etc., before considering ethical principles such as *Promises ought to be kept*.

Those philosophers who hold ethical statements to be assertions fall into two groups. Some hold that any ethical statement asserts something which cannot be asserted by means of any statement not containing an ethical word. Others hold that a statement not containing an ethical word can be used to assert the same thing. Let us call these Ethical and Non-ethical Assertive theories respectively. Those who hold that *You ought not to kill* means *It is God's will that you do not kill* hold a Non-ethical form of Assertive theory. Those who hold that what it asserts cannot be asserted by any other statement or can only be asserted by statements containing other ethical words such as *You are under an obligation not to kill* or *It is your duty not to kill*, hold an Ethical

---

[7] Prof. Ayer writes: "Sentences which simply express moral judgements do not say anything. They are pure expressions of feeling and as such do not come under the category of truth and falsehood." *Language, Truth and Logic*, p. 161. If the argument is that *because* they do not come under the category of truth or falsehood, *therefore* ethical statements do not say anything, there is confusion. If the argument is that *because* they are pure expressions of feeling, they do not say anything, there is not.

[8] I take the term *expressive* from W. F. R. Hardie, *Naturalistic Ethics* (British Academy Lecture, 1947), p. 27. It is not in all respects adequate, as will appear later, but it is difficult to think of a better term.

form of the theory. On this view the Naturalistic form of the Assertive theory will be one form of the Non-ethical.[9] It is plain that there will be corresponding Ethical and Non-ethical forms of the Expressive theory. I may hold that what is expressed by *You ought not to kill* is expressible also by *Don't kill* : or I may hold that what it expresses is not expressible by any other statement or only by a statement containing an ethical term. I have stressed this point because it is sometimes assumed that Expressive theories are necessarily Naturalistic. Perhaps the term *naturalistic* has sometimes been so used or defined as to imply that any one who held, for example, that ethical language expressed a peculiar moral emotion which could not be expressed without that language held a naturalistic theory of ethics. If so it is unfortunate, since it obscures an important distinction.

The simplest Expressive theory is that which has been variously designated the Exclamatory, Interjectional or, as I prefer to call it, the Pure Emotive Theory.[10] The theory arises, historically, from the distinction drawn between the logical and the emotive use of language. If we assume rather hastily that the logical use of language is to make assertions and the emotive is to express our feelings, it is

---

[9] To speak of Ethical and Non-ethical forms of ethical theory is a little confusing. Perhaps it would be better to coin two new technical terms and speak of Idio-generic and Hetero-generic theories. Mr. Duncan-Jones refers to what I have called the Ethical form of theory as the " distinctive concept " theory (" that at least one concept is involved in the analysis of moral judgements which is not involved in the analysis of any other kind of judgement "— Review of C. L. Stevenson's *Ethics and Language*, MIND (1945), p. 372). It is only by an ambiguity that this term would apply to both assertive and expressive theories. On the assertive theory moral judgement is analysed to involve a distinctive *concept*: on the expressive theory it is analysed (in an extended use of the word analysis to include explaining the use of non-assertive sentences) to involve a distinctive *attitude*. Of course, in the latter case also, the analysing involves a distinctive concept, viz., the concept of the distinctive attitude. I can express the distinctive attitude in a moral judgement without having a concept of it : but I cannot state what I am expressing without having a concept of it. A concept of a distinctive attitude would be, I think, a distinctive concept. Non-ethical forms of theory might be classified into naturalistic and transcendental : but there are probably many more categories. The whole concept of " the natural " would need to be clarified before it could usefully be employed to throw light on ethics.

[10] A. J. Ayer : *Language, Truth and Logic*, ch. VI. Perhaps no philosopher has held the theory in the " pure " form in which I state it, though some have sometimes spoken as though they did. Ayer combines it with other theories.

tempting to suppose that all linguistic utterances are either assertions such as *My watch is not going* or exclamations such as *Oh!* or *Alas!* or some combination of the two which it is the philosopher's business to unravel.

In its simple form the Pure Emotive Theory regards an ethical statement as made up of a non-ethical assertion and an ethical word having the force of an exclamation. The primitive ethical utterance would not even have the form of a statement, and would not include an assertion. Suppose I catch some one in the act of taking money which does not belong to him, and as I take in the situation, I utter a shocked *Oh!* Here the exclamation or interjection expresses an emotion directed towards the act taking place. Or I might say: "You are taking his money!" with growing horror in my voice. Then the theory is that, when I say *It is wrong of you to take his money*, I am asserting that you are taking his money and expressing my horror. There is clearly a parallel between these instances and instances which no one would consider ethical. I may exclaim *Oh!* with disgust at the soup in front of me: or I may say "This is mulligatawny soup!" with disgust in my voice: or I may say "This mulligatawny soup is awful." The Emotive Theory in its non-ethical form takes this parallel at its face value; and is not concerned to distinguish between the emotions in the ethical instance and in the taste instance. It is represented in its crudest form amongst non-philosophers by those who conclude an argument on morals by saying: "Well, you like telling the truth, I don't: and that's all there is to it." The ethical form of the Pure Emotive Theory can allow that, though there is a parallelism between the ethical instance and the taste instance, there is a significant difference in the emotions involved. It can say that ethical statements express moral approval or disapproval, two emotions not to be confused with liking and disliking or with other pairs of emotions expressible in non-ethical language. In using the term *moral* of the two emotions we should be using it simply to describe the peculiar nature of the emotions.

Before passing to an objection which applies to the

theory in either its ethical or its non-ethical form, I think it worth while to point out that the analysis into a non-ethical assertion plus an exclamation does not apply equally well to all ethical statements. Consider the statement *You ought not to take that money.* There is no non-ethical assertion, and what is more, no action in existence to provoke the exclamation. Perhaps this is not a serious difficulty. The poet Crashaw expressed " Wishes to His (Supposed) Mistress." Why should I not express disapproval at your (supposed) action? It would, however, be unplausible surely to suggest that I was expressing *actual* disapproval at your *supposed* action. It would be still more unplausible to suggest that I was feeling and expressing supposed disapproval: that seems nonsensical. The most plausible suggestion is that I am expressing disapproval of the kind of action. But even if this is so there remains the difficulty that I am not making any non-ethical assertion. I do not say that you have taken, are taking or will take the money: and I do not see what else I could plausibly be represented as saying. I conclude that the analysis of an ethical statement into a non-ethical assertion plus an expression of emotion breaks down.

What I think to be a fatal objection to the Pure Emotive Theory has been stated by Mr. Carritt.[11] I shall try to state it in my own way, because I have my own particular axe to grind. The Pure Emotive Theory is clearly to be distinguished from the subjective form of Assertive Theory which holds an ethical statement to be an assertion that the speaker is having a certain emotion. If the Pure Emotive theorist holds that the ethical statement *You ought not to take that money* expresses an emotion he must hold either that it is an involuntary symptom of an emotion, as bursting into tears is of grief; or that it is a voluntary attempt to convey or communicate the emotion. The former is too unplausible to be maintained: the latter is the subjective form of Assertive Theory, that ethical statements assert that the speaker is having a certain emotion. The unplausibility of

---

[11] E. F. Carritt: *Ethical and Political Thinking*, p. 32. He is criticizing the Pure Emotive Theory as held by A. J. Ayer.

the former interpretation may be seen by comparing two occurrences. If I discover some one to have taken money belonging to another I may say slowly, as I take in the situation : " You-took-that-money ! " and my voice may involuntarily express horror. If I say *It was wrong of you to take that money*, I clearly intend by using the word *wrong* to convey something.

Let us try to be clear on this point. Exclamations such as *Oh !* and *Ah !* may be involuntary symptoms of emotion, as tears : or they may be quasi-voluntary expressions, as when a child jumps for joy and shouts *Oh !* to himself. Again, an exclamation may be not merely voluntary but purposive, as when a farmer shouts *Hey !* to scare cattle from a field. If he shouts *Hey !* to some boys, then we have not merely a purposive utterance but a communication. The word is intended, not merely as with the cattle, to *scare* them off, but to *order* them off. It is true that what he says is logically inarticulate. If, instead of shouting *Hey !*, he shouts *Get off my land !* he communicates more clearly, because he articulates his command. We must not suppose that the logically articulate is co-extensive with the assertive, and the logically inarticulate with the non-assertive, forms of utterance. The instructions of a Government Department are no less commands than the barking of a Sergeant-Major.

It seems clear that, in *You ought not to take that money*, the word *ought* has communication value, and is not merely an expression of emotion. I do not wish to deny that it does express an emotion. In one sense of *imply*, the statement *You ought not to take that money* implies disapproval or some hostile emotion. When we use *imply* in this sense we mean, I think, that the emotion is expressed unintentionally and incidentally.[12]

Let us consider the statement *You ought to go to the meeting*. If it merely implies disapproval and does not assert that the speaker disapproves, and moreover does not assert anything

---

[12] Cf. G. E. Moore in *The Philosophy of G. E. Moore* (ed. P. A. Schilpp), pp. 540-3. I would say that *I am pleased you did X* expressed my approval by asserting it ; whereas *You did right in doing X* expressed my approval by implying it.

else, what does it say? The possible forms of theory, if we rule out, as I think we must, the Pure Emotive Theory, can be deduced by asking: In how many ways can A say something to B without asserting anything? There are, I think, five main communication-forms apart from assertions:—

(1) Commands.
(2) Promises.
(3) Questions.
(4) Declarations of intention.
(5) Wishes.

Declarations of intention and wishes differ from commands, promises and questions in that they need not be addressed to another person. This is why you can have an unexpressed wish or an unexpressed intention, but you cannot have an unexpressed command, promise or question.

There is a plausible case to be made out for the theories (1) that ethical statements are commands, (2) that they are wishes and (3) that they are declarations of intention. Before examining these theories I must digress to point out an impropriety in the classification of theories as Assertive and Expressive. This classification is based on the assumption that statements either make assertions or express emotions. We have concluded that, if statements express emotions they do so either by asserting the occurrence of the emotion in the speaker, e.g., *I feel horrified at your taking the money*, or by implying it, e.g., *You ought not to have taken the money*. If we refer to the theories which regard ethical statements as commands, wishes or declarations of intention as expressive, it is in a somewhat misleading sense that we do so. For there is no one thing which commands, wishes and declarations of intention all do and assertions do not do which can be called expressing. All, including assertions, express something in the sense that they logically articulate a certain possible state of affairs, e.g., B's going to the meeting.[13]

---

[13] If there is room for the technical term *proposition* it would best be used to denote this element which may be asserted, commanded, questioned, wished for, etc.

This may be asserted to be the case or commanded or wished by A or declared to be his intention by B.[14]

The sense, then, in which, on the Pure Emotive Theory, ethical statements are said to express emotion is not the sense in which a sentence such as *If only I were going to the meeting* expresses a wish. Hence a proper classification of theories needs to distinguish the Pure Emotive Theory on the one hand—which holds an ethical statement to consist of a non-ethical assertion combined with a merely inarticulate expression of emotion—from the group of theories which allow that the ethical statement is a logically articulate whole. As well as the theory that ethical statements are assertions this group would include the theories that ethical statements are declarations of intention, commands, or expressed wishes. Let us see if any of these theories have any plausibility.

The notion that an ethical statement declares an intention or expresses a decision[15] is likely to occur to us in two

---

[14] As the sentences *I am ill* and *J'ai mal* say the same thing by making the same assertion, so there may be sentences which say the same thing by asking the same question, by issuing the same command, making the same promise, expressing the same wish. Let us distinguish the command from the imperative sentences, the assertion from the assertive sentences, the wish from the optative sentences, etc., and refer to the sentences as imperatives, assertives, optatives, etc. Then an assertive makes an assertion. It may also imply an emotion: and the way in which an assertive implies an emotion is *somewhat* like the way in which tears express or imply grief or *Oh!* may express delight. An assertive may also imply the speaker's belief in the assertion made. An imperative issues a command. It may also imply a wish on the speaker's part that what is commanded be done. An optative, however, expresses a wish in the way in which an imperative issues a command and in which an assertive makes an assertion, not in the way in which tears express grief or a command implies a wish, i.e., it logically articulates the wish. It may, of course, *imply* anger or resentment. We speak of expressing a wish and declaring an intention, but not of expressing or declaring a command, a question or a promise, because there can be no command, question or promise unless it is logically articulated. That is why, when Hippolytus, in the play of that name by Euripides, says: η γλωσσ' ὀμώμοχ' ἡ δὲ φρὴν ἀνώμοτος (My tongue has promised, not my mind), he is guilty of flagrant sophistry.

[15] This view has been suggested by K. R. Popper, *The Open Society*, vol. I, ch. 5, and M. Macdonald, in an interesting paper, "Natural Rights," *Ar. Soc. Proc.* (1946-7). I think Miss Macdonald may be confusing *expressing a decision* with asserting that one has decided to do so-and-so when she says: "I will plunge, and say that value utterances are more like records of *decisions* than propositions. To assert that 'Freedom is better than slavery' or 'All men are of equal worth' is not to state a fact but to choose a side. It announces *This is where I stand*" (op. cit. pp. 243-4). A record of a decision would be an assertion of the kind "I decided to steer North North West."

ways. We may reflect on the kind of deliberative process which culminates in the statement *I must go*, said with an air of finality. Or we may reflect on the way in which we say to ourselves *Promises ought to be kept*. There is some plausibility in supposing that in the one case I am declaring a particular intention, in the other a general intention or policy.

Clearly, however, I do not always use ethical language to declare my intentions. I use expressions such as *I shall go* or *I shall continue to keep my promises*. What, then, is peculiar about the kind of intention which is declared by the use of ethical terms such as *ought* and *duty* ? Now the moment we try to answer this question we find ourselves back in the old familiar ethical controversies of traditional ethics. We might hold that it is an intention which consists in making up my mind to do what on the whole I want to do, after taking into account all my wants and the cost of satisfying them. In this way we could do justice to the undeniable difference between the intention declared by *It is my duty to go* and that declared by *I shall go*. The latter could be used to declare any kind of intention, the former only an intention of the kind described. Such a theory would be naturalistic, since it makes the peculiarity of the intention declared by the use of ethical language to consist in its character as a " total want," not in its manifesting any special moral component of our nature. We might, on the other hand, hold that the intention declared by ethical language was one formed after a process of deliberation which involved our being moved in a way not properly described as wanting. It is not my purpose to argue the merits of naturalistic and non-naturalistic theories of ethics. I merely wish to point out that an expressive theory of ethics does not liberate us from the choice.

To regard ethical statements as commands[16] does not differ greatly from regarding them as declarations of intention. If anything, it is rather more plausible. On the latter theory it is difficult to see how statements in the second

---
[16] R. Carnap, *Philosophy and Logical Syntax*, p. 24; A. J. Ayer, *Language, Truth and Logic*, p. 160.

person declare intentions. *You ought to go to the meeting* clearly does not declare an actual intention. It is not very plausible to regard it as declaring a conditional intention such as *I would go to the meeting if I were you*. It is worth remarking that this last sentence, though ostensibly saying what I would do in your position, is in fact used, if not as a command, at least as a plea. I have no doubt that ethical statements in the second person have an imperative character. I have little doubt that ethical statements in the first person have a quasi-imperative character. When I say to myself *I ought to go* I am in some way telling myself to go. But it is not so easy, on the command theory, to say what is happening when I say *He ought to have gone*. Perhaps the most plausible suggestion is that I am inciting others and myself to feel in an unfavourable way towards his not having gone.

The command theory must provide some account of the difference between commands which require to be expressed in ethical language and other commands. It is, I think, from a desire to do justice to the relative mildness of the ethical command compared with the forcefulness of a command such as *Get out of here!* that the suggestion is made that ethical statements are not commands, but wishes.[17] But the distinction between commanding and merely wishing is irrelevant. I may express a wish because I have not the strength to issue a command. I have non-ethical language to hand for either purpose. The use of ethical language clearly indicates some further fact.

I think the further fact is not hard to find. A pure command proffers no reason. The speaker relies on his own strength or the habitual subservience of the other person. The ethical statement proffers a reason. It is tempting at this point to fall back on the Assertive theory and say that the ethical statement *You ought to do so-and-so* both issues a command and asserts a fact. But how is this possible? We may hold that *You ought to keep your promise* says *Keep your promise* : then it is a command. Or we may

---

[17] R. Carnap, op. cit. p. 24. Carnap does not distinguish between saying that ethical statements are commands and saying that they express wishes.

say it asserts a fact. But we cannot say it says *Keep your promise because you ought to keep your promise* : for in this way we are introducing the command over again in allegedly giving the reason for it. Suppose we say that what it says is *Keep your promise because it is your duty, or it is right for you, to do so* we are no better off, though we avoid a formal difficulty of analysing an *ought*-statement into itself plus a command, because *It is your duty, or it is right for you, to keep your promise* has the same imperative force as *You ought to keep your promise*, and the difficulty would repeat itself when we came to analyse this statement into a command plus itself as a reason for the command. If we adhere to the Assertive theory we must give up the notion that *You ought to keep your promise* is a command. We may, of course, hold that it is an assertion made in the hope that the person addressed will be moved to keep his promise by believing it.[18] It is an attempt to move him by making an assertion. When Adam Smith said to Dr. Johnson : " You are the son of a bitch," he was making a false assertion to move the bear to display annoyance. Any assertion may, given suitable conditions, be used emotively, i.e., to provoke emotion.[18a]

We need not, however, fall back on the Assertive theory. It is not really plausible to maintain that we give someone as a reason for keeping a promise a fact asserted by *You ought to keep your promise*. But we do say *You ought to go to the meeting because you promised you would*. Here we have a command with a reason attached. It may be that the peculiarity of the ethical command lies in the reason given.

---

[18] " And if the form of words ' you ought to do so-and-so ' may be used as a way of inducing the person addressed to behave in a particular way, that does not in the least imply that the apparent statement is really not a statement, but a command. What distinguishes its meaning from the genuine ' do so-and-so ' is that one is suggesting to the person addressed a *reason* for doing so-and-so, viz., that it is right." W. D. Ross, *Foundations of Ethics*, p. 34. " There is no (discovered) reason in the world why a philosopher should not sometimes assert a true proposition which is also moving." Virgil C. Aldrich, *Some meanings of Vague*, in *Analysis* (1936-7), pp. 93-4. Or anybody.

[18a] " To assert that ' the country is going to the dogs ' does not provide determinate information concerning national events. It expresses primarily what the speaker feels about these things. But the statement does concern events the characters of which are very broadly sketched." C. A. Mace, *Representation and Expression*, in *Analysis* (1933-4), p. 34. Perhaps we might say that Adam Smith's statement concerned " events the characters of which were very broadly sketched."

Let us call commands which proffer reasons persuasives. Persuasives are of two kinds, which we may call suggestions and exhortations. The word *ought* is common to both kinds. Suppose I say *Since you want to be amused you ought to go to the Palladium*. Then I suggest you go ; I give as part of the reason for the suggestion that you have a desire to be amused; and I *imply* as a further part of the reason that whoever goes to the Palladium will be amused. Suppose I say *If you want to be amused, etc.*, then the suggestion is a conditional one. As it may not apply to you, the statement has much less suggestive force, and may be used to assert what it, strictly speaking, implies, i.e., *Whoever goes to the Palladium will be amused*.

On this account, *You ought to go to the Palladium* is not an assertion. Yet we are inclined to say that from *Whoever goes to the Palladium will be amused* and *You want to be amused*, it *follows* that *You ought to go to the Palladium*. This is an attempt to represent a practical suggestion and the reasons given for it as the conclusion and premises of a theoretical argument. To treat it as an argument is misleading. For what fact could be asserted by *You ought to go to the Palladium* ? Not that you *will* go. Still less that you *must*, i.e., will be necessitated to, go. If we insist on maintaining that a fact is asserted, we shall have to maintain that it is a fact consisting in a special kind of non-moral obligatoriness, since clearly it is not a moral obligation. This seems to me highly unplausible.

Here, then, is a use of *ought* in which it clearly has the force of making a practical suggestion. It is not a moral *ought* and the statement containing it is not an assertion derived as a conclusion from premises. Nevertheless, to make a suggestion and give reasons for it is in some respects like arguing and in some respects like commanding, though it is not either. For the person addressed is not condemned either to obey or disobey ; he can challenge the reason given by saying *I've heard that the Palladium is not very amusing* or he can deflect the suggestion by saying *I don't want that sort of amusement*. It is because he can take the latter course that there is significance in the non-moral *ought*. If, when a man said *I want only to be amused*, he had a perfectly precise concept of amusement and wanted anything that was an instance of it or a means to it, the appropriate answer would be *The Palladium is amusing*. It would be pointless to *suggest* anything to him. It is because the object of his desire is not conceptually determinate that there is scope for making a suggestion which he may or may not accept. If he accepts it, he not merely takes now a means to an end previously adopted ; he specifies his end in the process of taking this means. In other words, he chooses.[19] What he does at another's suggestion, he may do at his own suggestion. The process which goes on, when a man considers suggestions, whether his own or another's, and comes to specify what he wants more precisely, is a kind of thinking. It is rightly called practical thinking since it is unlike deduction or induction in having as its upshot not an assertion but a choice. We speak of it sometimes as deciding or finding out what one really wants, but it is not ascertaining a fact, it is specifying, i.e., making more specific, a want.

At the cost of a digression I must make good this last statement. Since my wanting something includes as part of itself my knowing what I want, " finding out what I really want " cannot be literally ascertaining what I am wanting. Of course, I may " want something without knowing what it is I want " : but in that case what I am wanting is just " something." I know no more about it. It may be said that I may know what I want without knowing exactly what I want. But then I am not wanting exactly that, though I may come to want it. I *can* literally ascertain what some one else is wanting, because his wanting something does not entail my knowing what he wants as it entails his knowing what he wants. Suppose I want to eat a banana, without having considered the fact that bananas

---

[19] Aristotle was right in connecting choice with deliberation, and therefore taking choice to be concerned with means. What he failed to realise was that deliberation includes not only inductive reasoning about what causes what, but dwelling upon new features which this reasoning reveals will characterise reality if this or that means is taken, and as a result coming to choose the-end-specified-by-this-means rather than the-end-specified-by-that-means. Choice, in other words, is of this-means-to-my-end : and this involves that in choosing I make my end more determinate and, perhaps, even change it.

may be green, yellow or over-ripe. I reject a green and an over-ripe banana when offered with the remark : " I want a ripe one." I specify my want because I have come to have a more specific want. Further specification may follow. The process may be performed by considering varieties of banana in the imagination. In the end I may conclude that I don't really want a banana at all. If the transition comes about gradually I shall probably say that I didn't really want a banana after all. If it came about suddenly, e.g., if I said " I want a banana " and then, when some were brought, said " No, I don't " I should say that I had changed my mind.

This process, which we call " finding out what we really want " we also call " making up our mind what we really want." If I am right, the latter is the more correct description : but the former emphasises correctly that, in making up our mind, we do so by finding out facts and marshalling them, as it were, before our mind. To represent me, when I ask myself what I really want, as trying to ascertain what I would want (i.e., be necessitated to want) if I were to consider facts I have not considered, is to mistake the question I ask myself. It is a practical question, viz., " What *shall* I want, in view of these facts ? ", not a theoretical question " What *will* I want, when I consider these facts ? ", which is asked and answered when I " find out " or " make up my mind " what I really want. If the theoretical question is not nonsense—and I suspect it may be—at least I find out what I will want in certain circumstances only by making up my mind what to want under those circumstances.

Consider now the ethical *ought* in the example with which I opened, *You ought to go to the meeting, since you promised you would*. It is a persuasive, not a command, since it is fortified with a reason. What distinguishes it from the non-moral *ought*? It exhorts, it does not suggest. We may state the command theory in the form that ethical statements are exhortations ; and that exhortations are a peculiar kind of persuasive, the peculiarity residing in the three features : (*a*) that a reason is given ; (*b*) the reason is not the existence of a desire on the part of the person addressed ; and (*c*) the reason is one of a certain number which can be listed. But we still have to meet the objection that this form of theory can apply only to ethical statements in the second person. We can, however, broaden the theory so that it will explain all the forms of ethical statement by incorporating elements from the various theories we have considered. This composite theory I call the *Attitude Theory of Ethical Statements*, and I formulate it thus : *Ethical statements express attitudes. Ethical principles are affirmations, not assertions.*

First, let me explain broadly how I propose to use the term *attitude*. I may have a favourable or unfavourable attitude towards a kind of action. What distinguishes an attitude, *pro* or *contra*, from, say, liking or disliking, is that these latter are *not* directed to a *kind* of action. I may like helping people in trouble and yet dislike you or any one else helping such people. If I have a favourable attitude towards helping people in trouble, I help them myself, encourage you and others to do likewise, and am pleased if you do so. More formally : If there is a kind of action which a man has a disposition to do himself, to encourage others to do, and to feel pleased at, when done by others, then he has a pro-attitude to that kind of action. An anti-attitude can be defined similarly. There is one qualification to be made. A disposition to act in a certain way may be actualised in the form of an abortive tendency so to act : what we call either a temptation or a good intention. For example, irascibility may be actualised in the form of a temptation to be rude, generosity in the form of an intention to be generous, without any overt action. No doubt this only happens owing to the presence of a conflicting disposition.

Consider a pro-attitude. It has three components which will be expressed in varying degrees by the different forms of ethical statement. *You ought to go to the meeting, since you promised you would* expresses a pro-attitude towards keeping promises. It does so chiefly by exhorting ; the other components are implied. *I ought to go to the meeting* expresses an intention (or tendency) and at the same time implies approval.[20]

This theory offers a prospect of a plausible non-ethical form of expressive theory. It is not plausible to hold that *I ought not to be cruel* expresses simply dislike of acting cruelly, for two reasons : (1) I can add without contradiction *but I do like being cruel* ; (2) in the sense in which it expresses an anti-emotion towards *my* being cruel, it implies the *same* anti-emotion towards any one else's being cruel ; whereas *I dislike being cruel* does not imply *I dislike other people being cruel,* nor does *I like being cruel* imply *I like other people being cruel.* Consequently, it might be maintained that the attitude expressed by an ethical statement is a complex of constituents none of which is specially ethical. The difference between a simple liking and a moral liking would be that the liking is moral if it is accompanied by the other components of a pro-attitude. In this way, the attitude expressed by an ethical statement could, in principle, be expressed without the use of ethical terms. For example, *You ought not to be cruel* might have the force of *Don't be cruel, don't enjoy cruelty in others ; I don't.*

If we accept the theory, we might accept the attitudes as typically human and, in that sense, as norms. We all possess these attitudes because we all uniformly approve and disapprove; and they are the final court of appeal on moral questions. Not to have them would be to be less than human. The expression of an attitude would correspond to the assertion of a principle of reasoning in logic. *Promises ought to be kept* would be the most general expression of the attitude towards promise-keeping and would have the force of *If any one has promised anything, let him do what he has promised to do, approve when others do likewise, and know by these tokens that I, too, will do the same.* This statement would not be an assertion ; nor an exhortation for which a reason would be given. It would be the affirmation of a norm or practical

---

[20] It is a little difficult to fit statements such as *He did his duty in going to the meeting* into this scheme. I think we should have to hold either (i) that there is a fourth component in the attitude, viz., encouraging others to take pleasure in their fellowmen doing acts of this kind, and that it is this which is primarily expressed by the statement ; or (ii) that there is a second order attitude which consists in fostering in one's self, encouraging and being pleased to contemplate in others, the first order attitude, and that it is the second component of this second order attitude which is primarily expressed.

principle, corresponding in the world of practice to the affirmation in the world of theory of a theoretical norm such as *If all M is P, and all S is M, then all S is P.* The former tells you what to do, given conditions of a certain general character ; the latter tells you what to assert, given premisses of a certain general character.

On this view, the attitude expressed by an ethical principle is not a premiss in the practical reasoning, but is the principle of the reasoning. To say : *You have promised to go, and therefore you ought to go* will be to exhort to an action and give a valid reason for doing the action. If the person addressed is not convinced of the principle, i.e., has not the moral attitude expressed by *Promises ought to be kept*, he will be unable to follow the reasoning. There will be no room for argument about principles. Argument on ethical questions will cease, once all factual questions are decided, and what remains will be a difference in attitude, which no rational process can modify. Where there *is* agreement on a formula it will be because there is agreement over facts and coincidence of attitude.

There are two objections to this position : (1) To call the moral attitudes principles of practical reasoning is a difficult and not very plausible analogy. From any two attitudes there may arise a " conflict of duties " ; and it seems absurd to suggest that " practical " principles of reasoning should lead to " practical " contradiction. (2) The *ought*, when used in the second person, would at best serve the purpose of awakening in the other an existent attitude. Certain facts, however, suggest that ethical argument or deliberation directed towards changing the moral attitudes is possible.

To remove the first objection, we might seek to find a single attitude implicit in all the moral attitudes. Suppose I find some one quite insensitive towards my exhortation *You ought to go to the meeting since you promised you would*, I may make an appeal to him by saying *If the promise had been made by him to you, you would want him to keep it ; don't you see that you ought to keep yours to him ?* It may be claimed that the attitude implied in this appeal is *the* practical principle. This would not only rationalise the moral attitudes by subsuming them under a single attitude, but would hold out the prospect of deducing them from that one attitude. The moral attitude to cruelty might be regarded as arising as follows : (i) my natural dislike of suffering pain ; (ii) my imagining other people suffering pain ; (iii) as a result, I come to be averse to inflicting pain, even though (iv) I have a natural liking to do things that are painful to other people. My capacity to imagine another person's pain may be peculiarly human and connected with my being able to reason. In so far as this capacity plays a part in the arising of the moral attitude, that attitude is, in a very special sense, rational. In so far as the moral attitude, conceived in this way, is also in a manner a development out of my natural likes and dislikes, i.e., those which I have when I am born and before I am capable of reasoning or of imaginative sympathy, the theory is quasi-naturalistic. I have little doubt that such a theory contains an element of truth. But the principle *Do only what you would want others to do in the same circumstances* and the corresponding negative principle do not in fact suffice to distinguish those attitudes we call moral.

A man may dislike doing a certain kind of action, e.g., smoking, and may also dislike other people doing it, do his best to stop them doing it, and encourage them to dislike others doing it. Then he not merely dislikes smoking, he has an unfavourable attitude towards it. But it is not a moral attitude. Again, a man may like indulging in heavy drinking, and may be sociable enough to encourage others to indulge in it, and to take pleasure in their doing so. This is a favourable attitude towards, and not merely a liking for, drinking, but it is not a moral attitude. Universality, i.e., the doing or forbearing what at the same time one wants others to do or forbear, characterises all attitudes.[21] The differentia of the moral attitude must be sought elsewhere. I think we must admit that if there is to be a moral attitude, it must contain at least one peculiarly ethical component, viz., the pro- or anti-emotion which I feel when I contemplate actions of the kind in question.

---

[21] The first Warden of Durham University is said to have remarked to a student who was smoking : " Mr. So-and-so, I don't like smoking in my university." He was expressing an attitude but not a moral attitude. If we sometimes use this form of statement in moral matters, e.g., " I don't like stealing in this house," it is because we are falling back on our authority which we do when we think moral exhortation likely to be ineffective.

The Attitude Theory in its ethical form explains how ethical statements, though they are not assertions, may be significantly made by one person to another. But, in so far as it holds that " morality is more properly felt than judg'd of," it cannot explain how the moral attitudes can be changed by thinking about the situation. Holding both that a peculiarly moral feeling is involved in our moral attitudes, and that we do in fact resolve a " conflict of duties " by thinking about the situation, I shall try to arrive at some conclusions by considering the facts of moral deliberation. I shall call the kind of ethical theory that could be developed on the lines I suggest, Ethical Humanism.

In the first place, the moral attitudes, though more determinate than the abstract formulæ in which they are expressed, are not by any means determinate enough to be applied mechanically to any situation. I am resolved, let us say, to keep promises. But an occasion may arise when I have to ask : Is this a promise, since it created no expectations in the other person ? It is no good searching the principle to decide whether the term *promise* implies the arousing of expectations. The principle shares the indeterminacy of the attitude it expresses. If I finally decide to treat the case before me as a promise I acquire a more determinate attitude towards promise-keeping. I solve a moral problem by ethical thinking. My coming to have this attitude is my " finding out what I ought to do." Secondly, in rendering more determinate one moral attitude, I bring about changes in the others. If I decide to keep a promise to some one, even at the cost of serious suffering to a third person, it is not only my attitude towards promise-keeping that is modified, but my attitude towards causing suffering to others. To explain one's moral principles it is not enough to recite them, nor even to recite them in order of precedence. It is not always that I decide to keep a promise rather than relieve suffering, or vice versa. Degree is everything in morality. This promise may be kept though it cause some suffering and yet broken if it were to cause twice this suffering. To explain our attitudes we should need to explain how we would act in all kinds of situations. In practice we should find ourselves saying of some situation : " I don't know what my attitude would be ;

whether I should be inclined to keep the promise or to relieve the suffering." If, under pressure, I were to say "I think I would keep the promise," and if I had really thought about the imaginary situation as if it were a real one, then I should be not finding out what my attitude is, nor finding out some fact—"that in that situation it is a duty to keep the promise rather than relieve the suffering"—but acquiring a more determinate moral attitude.[22]

In these two processes—the refining and readjustment of the moral attitudes—I fashion my moral personality. Perhaps it is this which some philosophers have had in mind when they have spoken of morality as creative. I propose to speak in more pedestrian terms of the corrigibility of the moral attitudes. We can, I think, speak of the process whereby they are corrected as ethical thinking. Can we speak of it as ethical reasoning? We are tempted to do so by our use of the expression *reflecting on the situation and doing what on the whole we have the best reasons for doing*. If I do not approach the situation morally, however, thinking about what to do would lead me to a quite different but equally rational decision. I may want to be cruel to some human being but I fear the consequences, so instead I decide to do what I next most want to do, viz., to be cruel to some animal, thinking that I can evade any social consequences. But suppose the very thought of a sensitive creature suffering pain creates in me a reluctance to do either of the actions, I shall act quite differently. If there is reasoning, it is equally valid in both cases.

It seems clear that there may be a situation (i) in which there are several things I want to do, though I want to do

---

[22] For the reasons given I cannot agree with what Dr. Ewing says in criticism of expressive theories of ethics : " That in making ' ethical judgements ' we are at least claiming to assert what is true is surely obvious from a consideration of our psychological attitude when we make them. When I try to decide what I ought to do in a given case I am conscious of trying to *find out something*, not merely of resolving or wanting to do something, and ' to try to find something out ' is to try to discover what is true about it." *Subjectivism and Naturalism in Ethics*, MIND (1944), p. 123. I think Dr. Ewing has assumed too readily that to find out something is always to discover what is true about it. If I try to find my way out of a cave, I am trying to do something, viz., to get out of the cave, not to discover what is true about the cave, though no doubt I shall discover in the process a good many things that are true. If it is said that I am trying to find out " what steps must be taken by a person wishing to leave the cave," and that the answer will be in the form of a hypothetical assertion, true or false, I can only say that this seems to confuse trying to find out how to do something with trying to find out what is or is not, practical with theoretical thinking.

some more than others ; and a situation (ii), like (i), except that in addition I have a tendency towards doing something which I do not want to do at all. In situation (i) there is something which can be described as what I want to do most but nothing that can be described as what I want on the whole. There is possible in situation (i) a process, which I have already described, of " finding out " or " making up my mind " what I really want or really want most. In this situation such a process tends to pass imperceptibly into deciding what to do. The same process *may* take place in situation (ii) but I have still to perform a different process of deciding what to do, in which I consider my wants from a new standpoint, that of their moral relevance, as well as considering other facts, besides my wants, from the same standpoint.

If we speak of reasoning in the one case we must do so in the other. There will then be two forms of practical reasoning. What is valid by one will be invalid by the other ; just as valid induction is invalid deduction. But it is misleading to speak of practical reasoning. Reasoning there will be in both cases, viz., inductive reasoning as to the probable effects of acting in certain ways. But the practical thinking proper in either case will be a different process, in its essentials not unlike that of determining which is the heaviest of a number of objects by holding each in turn in the hand. " Does this feel heavier than that ? " I ask myself. The question I ask and answer is *about* the objects, but I answer it by means of my feelings after paying careful attention to the objects. Let us call the feelings pressure feelings. If I have the most intense pressure-feeling when holding X, I judge X to be the heaviest. But I do not argue: When I hold X I have the most intense pressure-feeling, therefore X is the heaviest. I judge by simply saying : X *feels* the heaviest. The process is not immediate. It involves close attention and repeated trials. The appropriate word for this kind of thinking is judgement. " Good judgement " is this ability in general. In the sphere of one's own wants such judgement is prudence ; in the moral sphere, moral judgement.

Moral judgement and prudence involve as well as inductive ratiocination, a thinking which consists in discriminating and paying attention to many features of a complex whole. The thinking in either case can lead to a different conclusion on the same facts because the discrimination and balancing of facts proceeds on a different basis ; in the one case, *desirability* as measured by my wants, in the other case, *obligatoriness*, as measured by my moral sensibility. Four features are to be noted about the latter. First, there are no fixed principles on which the judgement proceeds. Moral rules are practical principles or norms to guide our action ; but they are provisional conclusions of our moral thinking, not principles by which it is guided. Secondly, there are not two stages ; a stage of factual exploration followed by a stage of emotional response. The two processes go on *pari passu*. Thirdly, the " conclusion " of the reasoning is an attitude expressed by the statement *This is my duty* or *This is your duty*. Fourthly, the judging is neither deduction nor induction. Its results are neither certain nor probable assertions, but attitudes. Forming an attitude is a little like framing a hypothesis. All the facts must be taken into account. But it also differs. The attitude has not to fit the facts, nor even to reconcile all my moral responses (for that is impossible). It is the process whereby one feeling reaches a predominant position, as the features of the situation are passed in review and I respond emotionally to them. These morally relevant features include the effects of acting in one way or another upon the satisfaction of desires ; upon the engagements contracted, and other features. One task of the moral philospher is to classify the morally relevant features.

If it is objected that, in the absence of any principle, moral judgement is an irrational process and moral decisions are arbitrary, the criticism is too incautious. No doubt, regarded as deduction or induction, the process is irrational, i.e., does not conform to the canons of either procedure. But this is to judge it by inappropriate standards. If we are tempted to judge it by these standards, that is because we crave for deductive certainly in the moral sphere. We would syllogise people into behaving properly. Once we recognise the absurdity of this craving, we need not fall into complete scepticism. Moral judgement involves a kind of thinking which can be done well or badly, and deserves for this reason not to be called irrational, or even non-rational. The truth behind the charge of irrationality is that the moral sensibility is involved in moral judgement as its non-rational basis. We may urge that to reach warranted conclusions by deduction or induction involves premisses ultimately grounded on the non-rational basis of sensation. There is a difference, however. Sensation can, it is thought, reveal objective fact, whereas feeling can only display the subject's response to fact. I think we must admit that moral principles and theories have the authority only of our moral sensibility, not, like scientific principles and theories, the authority of what our senses directly reveal.

Is there any sense in which ethical statements can be said to be true or false? I think there is. In expressing a moral attitude towards a particular course of action, either by saying *I ought to do X* or *You ought to do X*, I should justify the attitude by referring to the factual characteristics of the action which made a total impression on my moral sensibility stronger than those of any other possible action. I should be implicitly claiming, though I should not be asserting, that the decision or exhortation will commend itself to any one who considers the facts and allows them to register on his moral sensibility. Suppose the decision is to break a promise in order to help an injured man. I should be making, for example, the claim that *even* people who affirm *Promises ought always to be kept* would, if they attended to the facts, be led, by means of the very moral sensibility which led them to make this and similar statements, to modify the attitude expressed. In a somewhat special sense of verifiable and unverifiable, I could hold that the statement was verified or falsified according as this claim was verified or falsified. But it would not be falsified merely by people disagreeing, since they might disagree because they had failed to consider the relevant facts; or because they had failed to consider them from a moral point of view; or because their moral sensibility was undeveloped. If ethical controversy is not to be a mere tug-of-war between one attitude and another, the facts must be known, there must be a moral approach towards them and a certain humility which allows the moral sensibility to be awakened to new facts. In general, when we speak of true ethical principles, we are claiming that the attitudes they express have survived and will survive the impact of criticism. Not all survive: and looking back we can say that the statement or principle was false. We can say it with a little more confidence of the principles we have ourselves discarded, than of the principles which other people oppose to ours, since there is less danger in the former case of our mistaking greater moral sensibility for greater moral obtuseness.

If the theory I have very inadequately sketched were true, what would be the task of the moral philosopher? Clearly over a wide area the moral attitudes of different people coincide. One important task of the moral philosopher would be to map the moral sensibility or, as it is usually called, to expound the principles of moral judgement. But he can do more. By imagining a moral situation, finding out what his attitude in the situation is and expressing that attitude in suitable words, he can correct his attitude, and so far as we follow him, our attitude. For, if the situation is a novel one, or he draws our attention to novel features of the situation, his finding out what his attitude is will in fact be his coming to have a new attitude, or rather, a more determinate form of an old attitude. It is by this sort of moral rehearsal that a philosopher seeks to persuade us that we should reject the principle *It is a duty to keep promises* and accept instead *It is a prima facie duty (or obligation) to keep promises*. If we accept the new formula it is because we have made the experiment in the imagination and have acquired the modified attitude.

This task of the moral philosopher is different from that of the preacher and the reformer. The preacher reaffirms ethical principles for the salvation of those who are in danger of not acting on them, as all of us are at times. His chief weapon is rhetoric, since his business is to get us all to heaven, rationally or irrationally. The reformer is like Abanazar in the story of Aladdin. He offers us new norms for old, and, like Aladdin's new lamp, the new is usually a more startling affair than the old. Though he does offer us reasons for the new attitudes he tends to lose sight of the reasons for the old. The philosopher's task is critical. His business is to make us aware of our moral attitudes and to refine and sharpen those attitudes. The changes he introduces in his own and, if he is successful, in our system of attitudes are in practice very small. It would be a gross confusion to call him a preacher or a reformer. Like both, however, he is using language normatively to express an attitude, not to assert a fact. The notion that the moral philosopher, in approaching his subject, must set aside his attitudes and seek only the " facts of morality " is a fantastic apriorism comparable only to the notion that the metaphysician, in approaching his study, must set aside the evidence of the senses to seek only the "facts" of the universe.

If this is true, a good deal of moral philosophy is reprieved from the sentence which the expressive theory seems to pass upon it. Analyses of ethical terms will be false or nonsensical. But psychological analyses may have some truth, taken as an account of the state of mind expressed by ethical language, though they are untrue taken as an account of a state of mind to which such language refers. Those who have maintained the indefinable nature of such terms will be, among Assertive theorists, nearest to the truth. They *are* indefinable ; but the reason is that they are not terms, not that they are terms referring to a simple characteristic. Much that is said about moral psychology will retain its significance as description.

I conclude, then, that an ethics without propositions, whatever its difficulties may be, does not involve the denial of moral obligation or the acceptance of scepticism about morality ; that it does not settle the issues between Naturalism, Rationalism and other theories ; and that it does not make nonsense of most moral philosophy, though it interprets its contentions in a new way. Still, I think it must be admitted that when such an ethics is accused of making morality subjective, there is a sting in the accusation. Subjectivism in ethics may mean that form of the Assertive theory which maintains that an ethical statement asserts a psychological fact about the speaker. An expressive theory of ethics is not subjective in this sense. In another sense of subjective we contrast mere opinion as subjective with warranted belief as objective, and our mere likes and dislikes as subjective with our more impersonal attitudes as objective. In this sense a non-ethical expressive theory makes morality subjective, while an ethical form of the theory makes it objective. But there is one sense in which all such theories are subjective. They make morality the expression of a purely human attitude and, in the last resort, an individual attitude. I may affirm my ethical principles, saying : " These are the principles which commend themselves to me when I try to solve the practical problems which confront me by scrutinising the situation and bringing my moral sensibility to bear upon it. In affirming them I claim that others who do the same will come to affirm these principles : and that the rest of my experience will only serve to confirm me in them. But I know that I have modified them in the past and suspect that I will have to modify them in the future. They have only the authority of my human nature, passionate and rational."

It might seem that if, as well as the moral sensibility, we were to suppose alongside of it a rational faculty of moral intuition with a corresponding objective fact, morality would thereby acquire a greater authority ; whereas, without such a supposition, it is left floating, like Mahomet's coffin, in mid-air. When I conclude *This is my duty* I should not be simply expressing an attitude, though I should be implying an attitude—hardly anything that has been said in this respect would need to be altered—I should be asserting a fact about the action. This might be true, and would have to be decided on epistemological grounds. But even if it were true, it would make no difference to the procedure of ethical controversy, since the fact could not be demonstrated except by drawing attention to the morally relevant features, and to convince another of its existence I should still have to awaken his sensibility. Nevertheless, it may be said, it would provide an objective basis for morality.

I think the Ethical Humanist might plausibly say in reply : " The demand for epistemological objectivity in ethics is the product of a desire to strengthen ourselves and others in our moral attitudes when we waver. But it is misguided. What we crave is a greater than human authority not an other than human fact. Such an authority can be found, if at all, only in God, certainly not in epistemology. The doctrine of objective ethical facts apprehended by an act of intellectual intuition, even if epistemologically sound, is ethically irrelevant. It is, to parody a phrase of Hobbes, ' the ghost of the doctrine of Divine Commandments sitting crowned upon the grave thereof.' "

ARE ALL PHILOSOPHICAL QUESTIONS QUESTIONS OF LANGUAGE?

I.—*By* Stuart Hampshire.

1. The typical philosophical question which constitutes the title of this symposium is naturally interpreted as a request for a clear statement, firstly, of the criterion by which we normally distinguish philosophical from non-philosophical questions, and, secondly, of the criterion by which we distinguish questions of language from questions which would not normally be described as questions of language ; the question is finally answered when we have decided whether, from agreed statements of the criteria which we apply in the normal use of these two expressions, it follows logically that any philosophical question must be a question of language.

In formulating a criterion for the correct use of an expression, the philosopher, unless he is introducing an entirely new expression or recommending an entirely new use for an old and perhaps discredited expression, must attend to the habits and conventions which actually govern its normal use. He must assume that there are some nuclear contexts in which normal users will agree that the expression is applicable, although there may be peripheral contexts in which its application would be widely disputed. At least one purpose of his formulation of a rule or criterion is to enable disagreements about the propriety of the use of the expression in peripheral contexts to be settled.

It seems to me that no very serious disagreements in fact arise now in distinguishing philosophical from non-philosophical questions ; at least there is a solid nucleus of questions which almost all philosophers in fact recognise as distinctively philosophical questions. Certainly there are border-line or peripheral cases of questions which some philosophers wish to include among the philosophical and which others wish to exclude ; and different criteria or definitions may be proposed in order to widen or narrow the use of the expression in these peripheral contexts. But the expression has a tolerably defiinite use or meaning, in the sense that the proportion of border-line to nuclear cases is not uncomfortably high. We can draw up a generally agreed list of persons properly called philosophers and a generally agreed list of the questions which they have tried to answer, and this list would be at least as long as the list of border-line cases. There therefore seems to me to be no very urgent need for a precisely formulated criteria of what is and is not a philosophical question.

But the expression " question of language " does seem to me in need of clarification, because, although it is now often used by philosophers, it seems to be used by them in many different senses, that is the proportion of disputed contexts of application to agreed contexts is so high that we cannot say with confidence that it has *any* standard or proper use. So I shall attempt to disentangle some of the different senses in which this expression is used ; and then, assuming that we generally agree in recognising a philosophical question when we meet one, I shall ask for a decision whether all admittedly philosophical questions are questions of language in *any* of the senses which I have suggested for this expression. (I cannot show that all philosophical questions *must* be or *cannot* be questions of language, unless I *define* both these expressions, which I do not propose to do).

2. The expression " question of language " is often loosely used in antithesis to the expression " question of fact." At first sight the implication of this use seems to me that all questions can be classified as either questions of language or questions of fact. But on closer investigation it is not clear in ordinary use whether the alternatives are intended to be complete and exclusive, that is, whether the same question can be described as partly a question of language and partly a question of fact. Some philosophers talk as if a question *must* be described as *either* a question of fact *or* a question of language, and cannot significantly be described as both or neither ; their arguments sometimes suggest that the distinction is *intended* to be exclusive, although they may admit that the principle of distinction has never

in fact been so formulated as to exclude border-line cases. But other philosophers and (I think) most non-philosophers generally use the expressions in such a way as to suggest that, while there are questions which are *purely* questions of language and also questions which are *purely* questions of fact, they wish to allow a third category which are both or neither ; that is, they do not intend the classification to be, even in principle, complete and exclusive.

It is not difficult to suggest a variety of types of question about which there would in fact be no general agreement in ordinary non-philosophical usage in describing them either as *wholly* questions of fact or as *wholly* questions of language. A few simple specimen cases. (*a*) I am hesitating whether to describe a flower as mauve or purple. Is this hesitation either purely linguistic or purely factual ? My decision will be affected both by what other people say about the colour of this and other flowers (facts about their use of the two words), and also by direct comparison of this particular flower with other flowers which I myself unhesitatingly classify as either one or the other. (*b*) I am arguing with someone about whether he really believes the political or religious doctrine which be professes, or whether he is, as we say, self-deceived and only pretends to himself that he believes. Our argument would probably develop partly as an argument about the criterion which we apply in the use of the word ' belief,' and partly as a so-called factual dispute about his probable behaviour and states of mind. (*c*) I am asked by the doctor whether my tiredness is mental or physical. Clearly the doctor is not professionally interested in clarifying a question of language, and in some sense his question is certainly a question of fact ; but I could not answer him satisfactorily without clarifying what looks like a question of language, namely, without establishing what criterion is to be used in distinguishing the ' mental ' from ' physical.'

I do not deny that, of each of these three specimen cases, one might properly decide that the question proposed is *more* a question of language than a question of fact or vice versa ; probably one could arrange these and perhaps almost any other suggested questions, in a roughly agreed order as being more or less linguistic, or more or less factual questions. My only contention is that, if we insist on a *complete and exclusive* classification into linguistic and factual, the ratio of doubtful or border-line cases to the cases which are generally agreed as either one or the other will be absurdly high; which amounts to saying that in ordinary usage the two expressions are in fact not used as relatively complete and exclusive antitheses ; they are not ordinarily used as polar terms in the same way as, for example, the words 'mental' and 'physical' ; the proportion of border-line cases to generally agreed cases is, in the classification of events as either mental or physical, though not negligible, *comparatively* low.

If therefore philosophers decide for their own purposes to introduce a definite criterion by which we can, in the great majority of cases, definitely discriminate a question of fact from a question of language, then they will be introducing a largely new use of these expressions ; and the statement "All philosophical questions are questions of language," if established by the application of this new criterion, will be largely uninformative. As so often before, they will be representing an abnormally restricted or expanded use of a familiar expression as a significant discovery. Then the only question which can profitably be asked is—What is the purpose of introducing this new and precisely formulated use of a familiar expression ? What problems or pseudo-problems is this new and more exact use intended to solve or dissolve ?

I have not in fact been able to find in the writings of those philosophers who might be expected to say 'All philosophical questions are questions of language' any precise criterion for the use of 'question of language.' What one does find instead are precisely formulated criteria for distinguishing between analytic and synthetic statements ; and this is the distinction to which most importance seems to be attached when philosophical questions are discriminated from other kinds of question. But can these two distinctions be interpreted as identical? For the proper answers to many so-called questions of language are certainly not always, or even generally, analytic statements—e.g., what one looks for in grammars and dictionaries are not, in the sense ordinarily prescribed, analytic statements. The usual answer to this objection is that there are some questions of language which are not empirical questions about actual usage in a particular language, and this sub-class of questions of language constitutes the class of properly philosophical questions; they are questions about language with a capital L, and the proper answer to such questions is never a synthetic statement about actual usage in particular languages or even a generalisation from such statements, but always definitions or analytic statements. 'Question of language,' in this use, seems to mean what is meant by 'question of definition.'

It now becomes clear how far the expression 'questions of language' is being stretched beyond its ordinary use by philosophers who say 'All philosophical questions are questions of language'; for in ordinary use one would be inclined to say that what one means by a question of language is precisely a question which can be answered, and perhaps can *only* be answered, by reference to lexicon, grammar or observation of people's normal linguistic habits; this might even be taken as the definition of 'a question of language' in the ordinary loose sense. The redefinition or expression of the expression by philosophers is achieved by the use of the word Language as an abstraction, so that statements about Language are allowed which are not empirical generalisations about a number of actual languages.

This extension of the use of 'questions of language' to include questions which certainly cannot be answered by the empirical study of the actual use of particular languages has been misleading, as unfamiliar uses of familiar expressions for philosophical purposes must always tend to mislead, unless the unfamiliar use is explicitly acknowledged. But the use of the word 'Language' in this unusual and extended sense in spite of the inevitable but always corrigible misunderstandings involved, may bring out some philosophical point which could not be made in any other way. Philosophers' re-definitions, or calculated disregard of ordinary usage, although they must always to some extent provoke misunderstandings, are held to be useful and justified if they also serve to remove misunderstandings arising out of ordinary usage. So the question at issue is—what philosophical point is made by speaking of philosophical questions as always questions of Language in an extended sense of the word Language—that is, in a sense in which the answer to a question of language is not simply a synthetic statement about the normal use of a particular language?

3. Most philosophers who might be expected to answer the title question affirmatively (e.g., Prof. Ayer in *Language, Truth and Logic* and Prof. Carnap in *Logical Syntax of Language*) have, I think, wanted to assert and emphasise of at least the four following theses.

(*a*) All problems, which would ordinarily be described as philosophical problems, disappear, or in fact cease to be regarded as problems, as soon as attention is drawn to some misuse of, or ambiguity in, the words or expressions used in the formulation of the problem.

(*b*) In solving or dissolving problems by this method of drawing attention to misuses or ambiguities of words in their formulation, it is unnecessary, if the problem is genuinely philosophical, to consider any matters of fact, other than (possibly) facts about the normal use of particular words and expressions.

(*c*) All questions normally called philosophical, if they are significant and answerable questions, can be re-expressed, and are more clearly expressed as requests for definite criteria of use, or definitions, of the terms which they contain.

(*d*) In so far as we succeed in formulating agreed rules of use for the expressions of our language, we will not want or need to ask philosophical questions.

Although I think most of the philosophers who would answer the title question affirmatively would probably assent to all four of these theses, they seem to me to be different and logically independent, at least in the sense that it is logically possible to deny any one of them and to accept at least some of the others, and to accept any one of them and to deny at least some of the others. In particular there are certainly some philosophers who would accept (*a*) and (*b*) almost without qualification, but who would either firmly deny (*c*) and (*d*), or who would only accept them with substantial qualifications. I think there are good reasons for qualifying and amending all four statements; but (*c*) and (*d*), unlike (*a*) and (*b*), seem to me so misleading as to be properly described as false.

(*a*) and (*b*) seem to be misleading in so far as they may suggest that, as a matter of fact, all or most of the more notorious questions of philosophy have their origin in, or are answered exclusively by reference to, muddles or paradoxes in the use of our ordinary spoken languages. The history of the subject shows that many of the most important philosophical problems have been suggested by, and solved by a clarification of new developments in the methods of the physical sciences and of mathematics. It could even be argued, as a matter of history, that almost all the major philosophical problems have had their origin in the changing methods of the physical sciences and of mathematics. Even philosophical questions about our perception of material objects were originally asked, and still continue to be asked, not only or even primarily because people noticed a not easily clarified ambiguity in the the use of the words ' see ' and ' touch ' and their equivalents in other languages; but also because people have been inclined to believe, or to assume, that the well-attested statements of physical science about the nature of material objects and of our sense-organs are incompatible with out ordinary non-scientific statements about the physical world; and they have therefore come to express doubts about, or dissatisfaction with, ordinary non-scientific statements. But probably most of those who would be inclined to say 'all philosophical questions are questions of language' would retort that even if it is true as a matter of fact that many philosophical questions have been suggested by, and refer to new methods in science and mathematics, and not solely paradoxes or ambiguities of ordinary language, these questions are still usefully and properly described as questions of language; for, whatever may be the historical and psychological facts about their origin, they can all be answered by drawing attention to confusions between the terminology of physical science and of ordinary language, or to confused descriptions in ordinary language of the syntex and vocabulary of scientific language; these philosophical problems cease to be regarded as problems when the essential differences between the language of commonsense and the language of science have been explained.

This (to me convincing) reply would be a typical example of the philosopher's extended use of the word 'language.' When we talk about the 'language of physical theory,' and even more if 'the language of physical theory' is contrasted with 'the language of common-sense,' we should in ordinary usage be said to be talking not about two languages, but perhaps about two *kinds of language*; and we would discriminate between these two kinds of language by reference to the different *purposes* for which they are used.

Consider a typical philosophical question—e.g., Can thinking be defined as sub-vocal talking or a set of movements in the brain and larynx? The philosopher will not be considered in any sense to have answered this question if he merely draws attention to standard uses of the word 'thinking' and its equivalents in other languages; the questioner is intentionally going *beyond* our ordinary use of language. Suppose the same questioner goes on to ask 'Can all so-called mental processes, and states of mind, be described in terms of publicly observable physical motions?'

Then it would be even more clear that he was not asking a question about the criterion which governs the use of a particular expression in a particular language but a more general question. There is a sense (the extended sense now established by philosophers) in which he might be said to be asking questions about Language with a capital L, and not asking questions about the standard or proper use of particular expressions in a particular language ; that is, he would be asking for a comparison between different kinds of language.

It seems to me undeniable that philosophers always have been, and still are, confronted with questions of this kind, namely, questions which cannot be interpreted as requests for the formulation of the rules of use of particular expressions in particular languages. But I think that some (certainly not all) philosophers who want to say 'all philosophical questions are questions of language' would say that these questions, which are requests for *comparisons* between languages or kinds of languages, are in principle unanswerable ; and they would probably go on to say that *therefore* they are not genuine questions, but are pseudo-questions or meaningless questions, though this inference seems to me dubious ;[1] or, if they did not say that they are literally unanswerable, they would say that the only possible answer is not the kind of answer which the questioner expects. The answer would consist in setting out the rules of use for a language which might be called a behaviourist language, and then prescribing rules for the translation of those sentences in our ordinary language, which would ordinarily be said to describe states of mind, into sentences of this constructed language ; and the answer would end by saying that this logical exercise is the only answer to the question ' Can all so-called mental processes, or states of mind, be described in terms of publicly observable physical

---

[1] Surely a question cannot properly be described as meaningless unless it can be *shown* to be in principle unanswerable ; that is, unless we can formulate the rules for the proper use of the words which are misused in the question. And not all unanswerable questions can in this sense be shown to be unanswerable ; and that is generally the point of posing them.

motions.' If the questioner is dissatisfied with this answer, he must be told that all philosophical answers—that is, answers which are not empirical or scientific—must be either prescriptions of rules for the use of particular expressions in a particular language, or prescriptions of rules for the translation of sentences of one language into sentences of the other ; and this is the thesis expressed in (c) and (d) above, which I wish to dispute.

If the questioner were dissatisfied with this kind of answer, as I think he almost certainly would be, how would he express his dissatisfaction? What more would he be asking? He would be asking for a *comparison* between the *purposes* for which these two languages are used or are useful, and he might express his dissatisfaction with this narrowly logical answer by saying :— ' I agree of course that we can construct a purely physical language, if we choose, and also provide rules for the translation of the psychological statements of ordinary languages with the physical statements of the constructed language.' I agree that it is meaningless to deny that this is logically possible unless we are referring to some further set of linguistic rules which forbid this translation ; in that case, by definition, we should not be concerned with two independent languages, but with the rules governing the use of psychological and physical statements within a *single* language. But, although I agree that we can (logically) use whatever language we choose, provided that we use it consistently, I proposed my question in order to discover why, that is, for what purposes, we prefer one language to another ; if you like to express it in that way, I was interested not in syntax but in pragmatics. I wanted the philosopher to tell me, not how we may translate psychological statements into a physical language *if* we choose, but why, for some purposes, we in fact choose not to translate. We are inclined to say that something is lost in any such translation ; we seem to be unable to communicate in the new language what we wanted to say, and succeeded in saying, in the old. I asked my question because I thought that it was part of the function of philosophy, as the study of language in general as opposed to the study of the grammar of particular languages, to state our intuitive dissatisfaction with such translations more explicitly; that is, the difference between the purposes which the grammar of the language of physical theory is designed to serve, and the purposes which ordinary language is designed to serve. For most of the traditional questions of philosophy can be re-stated as questions about kinds of language in this very general sense of the word. He would be dissatisfied, I suggest, only because he had been refused an answer to his philosophical question as a question of language *in the wider sense* of ' question of language '—that is, the sense in which a question of language is not necessarily a question exclusively about the rules prescribed for, or actually observed in, the use of a particular language.[2]

Questions which are properly called questions of language in this wider sense may certainly be answered in part by drawing attention to the differences in the use of, for example, the word ' emotion ' in a behaviourist language and in ordinary language; it may also be useful to try to formulate definitions of the word which may summarise its use in the two kinds of language. But this clarification by definition cannot constitute the whole answer, because it will always make sense to ask whether one definition is better, or more useful for certain purposes, than another; and in defending or attacking a choice of a particular definition or rule for the use of ' emotion,' we may use arguments which would not ordinarily be called *wholly* arguments about language, even in the widest of the now established uses of this word. We might appeal to two facts, or sets of facts, which would not naturally be described as *wholly* linguistic facts : (*a*) we might point to the fact that those who have been using (for example) the behaviourist definition of the word ' emotion ' have not in fact

---

[2] I have not space to try to analyse what arguments we use in showing that one kind of language is useful for one purpose, another for another. I have used the word " purpose " vaguely; perhaps it can be clarified. I am only concerned to assert that such questions are asked and sometimes (I think) answered. What kind of argument can show that such questions *cannot* be answered?

succeeded in formulating by the use of their definitions simple laws which can be used to predict and control experience ; or (*b*) we might point to the fact that the use of the word 'emotion' in the sense suggested has always tended to mislead and confuse people, perhaps because the word has become inseparably associated in their minds with different uses. Whether a particular way of talking and thinking is useful or misleading, whether the adoption of a particular set of definitions or conventions enables us to discover and communicate what we want to communicate, or whether it only suggests unanswerable questions, is in the last resort settled by experience and observation ; the test of whether the adoption of a certain rule for the use of a familiar expression is helpful or misleading is an empirical test—does it in fact mislead? Strictly it is not language which is clear or muddled, but we who are clear or muddled. There are many syntactical irregularities and ambiguities in our languages which do not in fact mislead or perplex people ; that some other irregularities and ambiguities do mislead, as we learn by experience, could properly be called as much a fact of human psychology as a fact about language; and it is to facts of this kind that philosophers must, and do, attend.

4. But the philosophers who would maintain theses (*c*) and (*d*) would deny that the empirical study of the comparative usefulness for different purposes, either of different kinds of language or of different rules of use suggested within the same language, is a proper part of philosophy. Questions which can only be answered by reference to psychology or to any other empirical science cannot, given their definition, be described as philosophical questions, since they are partly scientific, and in so far as they are scientific they cannot (logically) be philosophical ; they ought therefore to be described as partly philosophical and partly scientific. This argument depends on so defining or using the word 'philosophical' that 'philosophical' and 'empirical' are antithetical terms ; it implies that the answer to any *wholly* philosophical question must be an analytic statement or statements.

I do not intend to discuss the empirical question (largely a matter of history) of whether this use of ' philosophical question' to entail ' question answered by purely analytic statements ' is or is not in accordance with normal use (even supposing that there is a definite and well-established normal use); even if it is not in accordance with this use, there may be good reasons for adopting a more restricted use; and again it is the *reasons* which have led philosophers to recommend this use, which are important.

But when we ask for these reasons, a dilemma arises; while the sentence ' the answer to any genuinely philosophical question is an analytic statement," may itself be an analytic statement, the adoption of this convention may be recommended by philosophers in statements which are (in part at least) empirical and not analytic; but if it is so recommended, there is a sense in which the conclusion is incompatible with the arguments which are used to support it; for the arguments used to support this *philosophical* conclusion would contain *empirical* statements. If on the other hand the conclusion is supported by arguments consisting *wholly* of analytic statements, that is, if this rule for the use of the word " philosophical " is shown to be the logical consequence of other rules for the use of other expressions, it will still be possible to ask why we should adopt this whole set of rules or definitions. And yet anyone who attempted to answer would thereby forfeit the title of philosopher.

The reasons for classifying questions as philosophical only if empirical statements are not required in answering them are in fact more often implied than directly stated (perhaps in part to avoid this charge of inconsistency). The reasons usually given or implied are partly logical, and partly historical and psychological. The logical doctrine is (roughly) that all significant questions must be answered *either* by appeal to experiment and observation, or by appeal to definitions or axioms (and this thesis is usually presented as an analytic statement showing the proper use of ' significant'); the historical and psychological doctrine usually implied is that *in fact* philosophical arguments have in the past led to interminable misunderstandings largely because philosophers have generally failed to make clear, either to themselves or to others, which of the two kinds of question they were trying to answer ; we learn by experience that whenever the two kinds of question are carefully distinguished, philosophical perplexities tend to disappear and outstanding problems are seen to be soluble ; empirical questions are remitted to scientists for solution, and the remainder which can now be clearly classified as genuinely philosophical, are interpreted as requests for definitions or rules of use.

Whether or not philosophical perplexities do in fact tend to disappear and problems to be solved when, and only when, this method is used is surely an empirical question to be decided by experiment and observation of the results. Since the publication of Wittgenstein's Tractatus Logico—Philosophicus, the experiment has in fact been made and the results have in fact been generally favourable ; many misunderstandings have been clarified and many perplexities removed ; and precisely this *fact* is the best *reason* or *justification* for insisting on a clear distinction between a philosophical question and a scientific or factual question. The justification of the adoption of one method (or, in the wider sense, language) rather than another, in philosophy as in any other enquiry, is a pragmatic one—that, when we use it, we find answers to the questions which we want to answer. Conversely we call methods or terminologies misleading if we find that we are thinking to no purpose when we use them. And it is certainly true that philosophers have in fact been generally misled by failing to distinguish clearly in their manner of expression between empirical and non-empirical questions ; it is therefore, in a strict sense of the word, less misleading to distinguish clearly between the two kinds of question; and it is this point which philosophers have wished to stress when so defining or using the word 'philosophical' that 'philosophical' and 'empirical' exclude each other, that a question cannot be both 'philosophical' and 'empirical.'

This neat classification of questions into philosophical and scientific is useful and even necessary, provided that that it is not so rigidly applied as to be made the basis of a new scholasticism. Like almost all such classifications of statements or questions into types or compartments, it is useful as a rule which throws into relief the exceptions to the rule. The rule has been used very effectively in the last twenty-five years as an axe to clear away the undergrowth of the tangled cross-purposes of a priori psychology called philosophy. But it may be useful now, when the reasons for saying ' no philosophical question is a question of fact ' are so widely appreciated, to emphasise the reasons for *not* saying it, to draw attention to the respects in which it may be (and I think already has been) misleading, and so to emphasise the exceptions to the rule. It is for this reason that I have emphasised the difference between proposing definitions, or rules of use, and giving reasons for preferring one set of definitions or rules to another, between showing that a certain use of language is self-contradictory and showing that it is misleading. If any one chooses to accord the title of philosopher only to those who are wholly engaged in the first of each of these activities, he will be adopting an abnormally restricted use of the word ; and, if he at the same time declares himself a philosopher, he will be unable consistently to provide any satisfactory reasons for departing so widely from normal use.

5. I think many contemporary philosophers would be inclined to say both (*a*) ' all philosophical questions are questions of language ' and (*b*) ' no philosophical questions are empirical questions ' ; given these philosophers' use of ' question of language ' to mean ' question of definition,' these two theses are logically equivalent. But if one considers (*a*) alone, as the title of this symposium requires, and disregards the abnormal use of ' question of language ' to mean ' question of definition ' a relevant historical parallel suggests itself. Philosophy was once conceived as the study of Reality, but was displaced by the application of empirical methods in the physical sciences ; it was also

conceived (by Locke, Hume, Kant, and so many others) as the a priori study of Mind with a capital M, or Knowledge with a capital K, but is being gradually but firmly displaced by the application of empirical methods in psychology; it is now generally conceived as the a priori study of Language. Surely it is reasonable to suppose that people will once again become discontented with a priori generalisations about an abstraction, and will turn to a methodical study of the facts, to comparative linguistics and semantics, only recently discernible as sciences. It seems historically to be the function of philosophy to initiate genuine science by speculation; in all its phases (outside pure logic) it is pre-science.

But, whether or not this prediction is confirmed, philosophers who claim that all philosophical problems are dissolved when attention is drawn to confusions and ambiguities in the use of words cannot reasonably neglect the comparative study of actual languages; they must ask whether particular metaphysical perplexities *in fact* only suggest themselves in languages in which particular grammatical forms and idioms are used, and whether some philosophical problems are *in fact* not felt to be problems, and perhaps cannot even be formulated, in languages which have very different grammars. Until this evidence is available, it is impossible to decide how many current philosophical questions can be said to be questions of language in the narrower sense, and how many are questions of language only in the wider sense. And if they do ask these questions, they will be asking questions of fact which are also (in the normal sense) questions of language.

6. To summarise :—

(a) No criterion has been suggested by philosophers with by which we can distinguish a question of language from a question which is not a question of language. In ordinary non-philosophical usage a pure question of language is generally a question which can be answered by observation of actual verbal habits observed in particular languages.

(*b*) But philosophers, for their own good reasons, have established a wider use of the expression ; in this wider but so far unformulated sense, a question of language is not necessarily a question about the proper use of a particular expression in a particular language. It has been found illuminating, although it also has sometimes been misleading, to describe a philosophical question as a question of language in this wider sense.

(*c*) Some philosophers would probably use the sentence ' all philosophical questions are questions of language ' to mean what is meant by ' no philosophical questions are empirical questions ' ; or ' all philosophical questions are questions of definition.' There were good reasons for suggesting this rule of distinction between philosophical and scientific questions ; but if one asks what these reasons are, one is asking a question which would ordinarily be called philosophical and which would (I think) ordinarily be called, at least in part, an empirical question, or which would ordinarily be said to *involve* empirical questions. Therefore the dictum ' all philosophical questions are questions of definition ' cannot be accepted. Probably no philosophical questions are *purely* empirical questions, and some philosophical questions are *purely* questions of definition, but certainly some philosophical questions are partly one, and partly the other.

The title-question is certainly a philosophical question, and my answer shows that I at least have interpreted it as *largely* a question of language, even in the narrower sense of the words ; and, in some extended but so far unanalysed sense of the words, I might be said to have treated the question as *wholly* a question of language. But I have made some statements which are certainly empirical statements ; and I think I can safely defy anyone to answer the question satisfactorily without making at least one empirical statement. Therefore my general conclusion is that, although one may say ' all philosophical questions are questions of language ' (in an abnormally extended sense of ' question of language '), a question of language, in this sense and in this context, may also sometimes be, at least in part, an empirical question. 'All philosophical questions are questions of language' is misleading if an identity of meaning is implied between 'questions of language' and 'questions of definition'; but this does seem to be implied in some of the arguments of some philosophers who would wish to maintain that all philosophical questions are questions of language.

II.—*By* Austin Duncan-Jones.

I shall assume, following what I think is Mr. Hampshire's procedure, that there is a recognised class of questions which may be called " philosophical," about whose membership philosophers are roughly agreed. New members of this class are discovered from time to time. But there is no agreement, nor is it easy to discern, what the defining characteristic is which qualifies a new candidate for admission to this class.

It is often suggested nowadays that the qualification is linguistic. I think Hampshire assumes that, in order to decide whether this is the case, the chief need is to decide what a question of language is, and that, could this mystery be solved, the rest would be easy. It seems to me that it is not very difficult to see what a question of language is, but that it is difficult to give an account of the nature of philosophical questions.

Hampshire rightly pays a good deal of attention to the peripheries of concepts. But I think he is sometimes haunted by them to a degree which prevents him from making any unqualified statement at all. By way of redressing the balance, I shall say as little as possible about marginal cases.

I am not sure which of the points which Hampshire raises he most wishes us to discuss. I think most of what I am about to say is relevant to one or another of Hampshire's points : but I shall not connect my discussion very closely with his.

(1)

There seem to be two main ways of interpreting the phrase " question of language ". We may take it as referring to the content of a question, or to the method of answering it. Of the former interpretation, which is perhaps the more obvious, Hampshire says nothing : his discussion turns entirely on the latter interpretation.

The results of classifying questions according to their content and of doing so according to the method of answering them will often, no doubt, coincide. " Where is the British Museum ? " is a question of geography, both in the sense that it contains the name of a place, and in the sense that its answer is to be found by getting information about places. But there seems to be no general reason for the two classifications to coincide.

I shall deal first with questions of language in the sense in which they are questions distinguished by a certain content. What I am about to say seems so familiar and obvious that I hesitate a little to devote space to it. But I can't find that Hampshire has taken note of the points which follow.

(2)

In the rest of this paper the words " question " and " problem " will often be used in special limited senses. These, and special uses of certain other words, I shall mark by initial capitals. By a " Question " I shall mean a sentence in interrogative form. When two Questions are equivalent I shall say that they are, or express, the same Problem. This relation of Question to Problem may also be expressed by saying that the Question is a Version of the Problem ; or it may be said that either Question is a Version of the other. Thus " what are numbers ? " and " was sind die Zahlen ? " are distinct Questions, but they are two Versions of the same Problem. One Question, I assume, may be equivalent to another without being, say, a translation from English into German. " What are your called ? " and " what is your name ? " are equivalent Questions.

In the four theses which he sets out at the beginning of his third section, Hampshire seems to distinguish tacitly between a " problem " and a " question "—at any rate, he uses only the word " problem " in theses (*a*) and (*b*), and only the word " question " in theses (*c*) and (*d*). I am not sure what distinction Hampshire has in mind, and I have no reason to think it is the same as the distinction which I have just drawn.

Sometimes there is a set of two or more Questions which are so interrelated that each can serve many of the purposes that each of the others would serve, and we pass insensibly from one to another ; and it might be admitted that certain Questions stood in this relation to one another even if it were denied that they were equivalent. Of such Questions, I shall say that each is a Variant of any of the others. I shall assume that if Questions are Versions of one another it follows that they are Variants, but that they might be Variants without being Versions.

Variants of a Version of a Problem may also be called Variants of the Problem. It follows that, while a Question can only be a Version of one Problem, it may be a Variant of several Problems.

It seems natural to call a Question a Question of language if it fulfils either of two conditions : namely, if it contains a name or description of an expression or class of expressions—more briefly, if it mentions expressions ; or if it is so phrased that any answer to it must mention expressions. " What does ' dog ' mean ? " fulfils the first condition ; " what are those barking things called ? " fulfils the second. Questions which fulfil either of these conditions I shall call Linguistic, and those which fulfil neither non-Linguistic. If all the Versions of a Problem are Linguistic it is natural to call the Problem a Problem of language : I shall say that such Problems are fully Lingual.

Fully Lingual Problems are plentiful. The Problems of which the two Questions cited in the above paragraph are Versions will serve as examples. In general, all Problems about the natural history of languages—Problems about etymology, grammar, meanings in the dictionary sense, and so on—are fully Lingual.

I shall assume that a Question exists if it is constructible : or in other words I am prepared to countenance subsistent Questions, like subsistent propositions.

I am sorry I have had to introduce so much special jargon. Perhaps with further thought it could have been reduced or got rid of : but writing under the usual pressure of symposium conditions I have not seen how to reduce it.

(3)

When a Question, whether philosophical or not, is non-Linguistic and puzzling, we are apt to replace it by a Linguistic Variant. When we are using words colloquially, we do not distinguish sharply between Linguistic and non-Linguistic Variants : we slip insensibly from one to the other. In dealing with Problems which are not fully Lingual, our choice of expressions is prompted, partly by attention to non-linguistic matters, and partly by a continuously variable degree of attention to the way in which we are expressing ourselves. In proportion as the subject we are dealing with is obscure, or highly abstract, or involves unfamiliar concepts, we are apt to distrust our settled modes of expression : and in proportion as we distrust our settled modes of expression we are apt to substitute a Linguistic Variant for a non-Linguistic Question—and to make a corresponding substitution among propositions.

What we do in such cases is to use a Linguistic Variant which refers to fittingness of language, containing such expressions as " might one say that . . . ", or " is so and so properly described as . . . ", or " would it be misleading to say that . . . ". These formulæ indicate that we are enquiring as to the appropriateness of some expression or class of expressions to some fact or class of facts. The expression in question is often mentioned autonymously and is written without inverted commas. I shall follow this practice when it seems convenient.

If Q is a non-Linguistic Question, we may write " Q_L " for a Linguistic Variant of it. (These symbols, and those which follow, should be regarded as abbreviations for unspecified expressions, rather than names of expressions.)

Suppose Q to be " is staying in bed a cure for a cold ? " Q_L might be " can staying in bed properly be described as a cure for a cold ? "

Here, and in many trivial examples, there is little motive for passing from Q to Q_L. But we could always do so in case of need, and we may therefore say that in a sense every Problem has Linguistic Variants. *A fortiori*, since most or all philosophical Problems are obscure, or highly abstract, or involve unfamiliar concepts, we may expect all philosophical Problems to have Linguistic Variants. I hope to avoid the mare's nest of proving that all philosophical Problems are Problems of language by proving that, in some odd sense, all Problems are.

Let us suppose that, in some undefined sense, no philosophical Problem is linguistic. There will none the less still be a tendency for Linguistic Variants of philosophical Questions to be used, and an illusory appearance of philosophical Problems being Linguistic will be created. We should therefore be guarded about accepting linguistic accounts of philosophy : for whether they are correct or not appearances will be in their favour.

(4)

It may be denied that a non-Linguistic Question and a Linguistic Variant of it are, in general, equivalent : but there may still be instances in which they are equivalent. For example, it might be argued that " what is an uncle ? " (used in a certain way) is equivalent to " what does the word 'uncle' mean ? " Let us suppose that there are such instances. Then there are some Problems which have both Linguistic and non-Linguistic Versions : and a given Problem may have no Versions which are Linguistic, no Versions which are non-Linguistic, or some which are Linguistic and some which are non-Linguistic. I shall call those of the first kind non-Lingual Problems ; those of the second kind I have already named fully Lingual ; and those of the third kind I shall call partly Lingual.

There are the following possibilities in respect of the Lingualness of philosophical Problems.

1. All philosophical Problems are non-Lingual.
2. All philosophical Problems are fully Lingual.
3. All philosophical Problems are partly Lingual.
4. Some philosophical Problems are non-Lingual, some are fully Lingual, and some are partly Lingual.
5. Some philosophical Problems are non-Lingual, some are fully Lingual, and none is partly Lingual.
6. Some philosophical Problems are non-Lingual, none is fully Lingual, and some are partly Lingual.
7. No philosophical Problem is non-Lingual, some are fully Lingual, and some are partly Lingual.

The eighth possibility, that there are no philosophical Problems, I shall not discuss.

I think it is unquestionable that there are Linguistic Versions of some philosophical Problems, and that there are non-Linguistic Versions of some. Possibilities (1) and (2) may therefore be dismissed. But I can't see any ready method of dismissing any of the other five.

I will assume for the moment that the word " question " in our title is equivalent to my " Problem ". If possibility (7) were realised, there is an obvious sense in which the answer to the title Question would be " yes ". If possibility (3) were realised, the answer might be " yes " : but some additional reason would then be needed for regarding the Linguistic Versions of a Problem as more essential than the non-Linguistic.

If possibility (4), (5) or (6) were realised, there is an obvious sense in which the answer would be " no ".

I do not see any ready means of proving that some one of these possibilities is realised. My excuse for setting them out somewhat elaborately is that, if we *could* give such a proof, it would, I think be a genuine contribution to the subject set before us by Hampshire's paper.

(5)

I come now to the second interpretation of the phrase " question of language ". The colloquial use of this and kindred phrases is elastic and subtle. Sometimes we say " that's a *mere* question of language ", or " a mere verbal question ", " a mere question of words "—for example, of the Question " is a lobster a fish or an animal ? " Or " a *purely* verbal question " (" is a parent's brother an uncle ? "). Or " partly a question of language " (" was the discovery of atomic fission a disaster ? "). Or, very often, " a question of language " without further qualification. It will not be possible here to go into the subtleties of natural usage, and my discussion will have to be somewhat crude and schematic.

By finding out what an expression means we may obtain either the whole or part of the answer to a Question. Suppose there is a Question, Q, of the form " is S K ? ", and a Linguistic Variant, Q_L, of the form " can S properly be called ' K ' ? " (" K " is an abbreviation for some name of a characteristic, and " S " for a name of some thing or class of things to which K might belong.) The answer to either of these Questions may or may not be obtainable by analysis of the meaning of " S ".

1. " K " may stand for a characteristic included in the meaning of " S " ; or for a conjunction of characteristics, all of which are included in the meaning of " S " ; or for an alternation of characteristics, at least one of which is included in the meaning of " S ".

2. " K " may stand for a characteristic not included in the meaning of " S " ; or for a conjunction of characteristics, not all of which are included in the meaning of " S " ; or for an alternation of characteristics, none of which is included in the meaning of " S ".

3. " K " may stand for a characteristic whose contradictory is included in the meaning of " S " ; or for

a conjunction of characteristics, the contradictory of at least one of which is included in the meaning of " S " ; or for an alternation of characteristics, the contradictory of all of which is included in the meaning of " S ".

In general, in order to answer Q_L, we must take two steps : first we must find out what characteristics " K " stands for, and then whether they belong to S. But in cases (1) and (3) above the second step is automatic. In case (2), on the other hand, the second step may require empirical investigation; or it may be obvious, not because " S is K " is analytic, but because its truth or falsity is well known.

The answer to Q, which may be called " A(Q) ", follows in a certain way from $A(Q_L)$, the answer to Q_L. For if S may properly be called " K " it follows that anyone who says that S is K speaks truly, and from that it follows that S is K.

If we are doubtful about both the steps in obtaining $A(Q_L)$, we shall probably say that Q is partly a question of language. Suppose Q is, for example, " was the discovery of atomic fission a disaster'? " and suppose we are uncertain both about the meaning of " disaster " and about the effects of the discovery. It seems curious at first sight that we are—as it seems to me—more likely to apply the description " question of language " to Q than to Q_L, although the latter is Linguistic and the former is not. This practice, which largely justifies Hampshire's ignoring of my first interpretation, no doubt arises from the fact that the reference to language in Q_L is obvious and needs no stressing, while it may not be obvious that a reference to language is relevant to answering Q.

I am going to assume that the first step in obtaining $A(Q_L)$ is always empirical : that is to say, that a proposition such as " ' K ' stands for C_1, C_2, etc." is always an empirical proposition, whether it is concerned with established usage or with some arbitrary usage. For example, when I say in my second section that by a " Question " I shall mean a sentence in interrogative form, I hold that I am expressing an introspective judgement about my own intentions.

When Q is wholly a question of language, in the sense just pointed out, A(Q) may be either analytic or empirical. (I am following Hampshire's example in assuming that there is no other kind of proposition we need consider.) Suppose Q is the Question " is staying in bed a cure for a cold ? " We all know that, on the whole, staying in bed does good to people with colds. But we might be doubtful about the meaning of " cure ". If we conclude that anything which, on the whole, does good to sufferers from a certain ailment may be called a " cure " for that ailment, $A(Q_L)$ is deducible, not from this conclusion alone, but from this conclusion in conjunction with matters of common knowledge.

But suppose Q is the Question " is a parent's brother an uncle ? " Then $A(Q_L)$ is deducible from the proposition which tells us the meaning of " uncle ", and A(Q), an analytic proposition, is deducible from the empirical proposition $A(Q_L)$. This strange and interesting kind of deducibility cannot be discussed here : I shall mark my sense of its oddness by a special name, and shall say that $A(Q_L)$ Validates A(Q).

The relation between $A(Q_L)$ and A(Q) has only been illustrated in the simplest case, in which A(Q) is a subject-predicate proposition. But whatever analytic proposition A(Q) may be, there will, I assume, be some empirical proposition, $A(Q_L)$, which Validates A(Q).

When Q is partly or wholly a question of language in the sense pointed out above, we may say that Q is partly or wholly Verbal. When A(Q) is empirical I shall say that Q is inessentially Verbal, and when A(Q) is analytic I shall say that Q is essentially Verbal. A Problem may be called essentially Verbal if some or all of its Versions are essentially Verbal.

I think one of the main Problems which Hampshire has in mind might now be expressed as follows. " Is every philosophical Problem either essentially Verbal, or a Problem whose Versions are Linguistic Variants of essentially

Verbal Questions ? " This looks unduly complicated, and the crux of the Problem lies, of course, in the first alternative. The second alternative must be included, because if Q, an essentially Verbal Question, is philosophical, we can hardly refuse to say that Q_L is also philosophical.

In recent times many solutions of philosophical Problems have been advocated, each of which, if correct, would imply that the Problem in Question was essentially Verbal. It has been implied that Problems about perception, induction, the self, time, and so on, can be solved by discovering what we mean, in this or that context, by such expressions as " see a penny ", or " good grounds ", or " I ", or " now ", and by that means alone : and that, given a correct account of this matter, one and only one correct solution is possible, on which no empirical evidence could cast doubt. The answer given is often of the form " in a sense yes, and in a sense no ". But this is equivalent to saying that a certain Question might be a Version of one Problem and might be a Version of another ; and that in one case the answer is " yes " and in the other " no ". Each of these answers will be analytic.

Let us suppose that many of these solutions are correct ; that their propounders have correctly answered some Linguistic Question, and correctly deduced from their answer an analytic proposition, which is the solution of a philosophical Problem. There is some danger of over-rating the linguistic element in what has been done. If we begin by considering Q, we shall not go on to consider Q_L, as a help to the solution of Q, unless we already have some independent insight into the nature of Q. If we have an inkling that A(Q) is analytic, we have a motive for looking for $A(Q_L)$, by which A(Q) will be Validated. But if we have a little more than an inkling, the motive disappears. Given sufficiently good intuitive powers, every essentially Verbal Problem could be solved without any reference to a Linguistic Variant, and such references would be superfluous except as an aid to exposition.

The doctrine that every philosophical Problem is either essentially Verbal, or a Problem whose Versions are

Linguistic Variants of essentially Verbal Questions, may be called Verbalism. If an advocate of Verbalism also held that the most profitable way of dealing with essentially Verbal philosophical Problems is always to consider Linguistic Variants, we might say that he was not only an ontological but also a methodological Verbalist.

I will return for a moment to the relation between the first and second interpretations of " question of language ". If Verbalism is true, and if, when Q is an essentially Verbal philosophical Question and Q_L a Linguistic Variant of Q, Q and Q_L are equivalent, it will follow that possibility (3) in section 4 is realised, that is, that all philosophical Problems are partly Lingual.

(6)

Verbalism might be proved either *a priori* or inductively. It would be proved *a priori* if we found that we were never prepared to give the name " philosophical " to a Question which satisfied neither of the conditions laid down by Verbalism ; that is, if Verbalism turned out to be itself analytic. It would follow, perhaps inconveniently, that we could never know whether an unsolved Problem was philosophical.

Verbalism would be proved inductively if we tried to answer a series of non-Linguistic philosophical Questions by finding some Linguistic Variant whose answer would Validate an answer to the original Question, and always succeeded in doing so. If the Problem whether Verbalism is true were itself philosophical, it would follow that our inductive generalisation had at least one exception.

Thirdly, Verbalism, though unproved, might be proclaimed as an expression of faith or hope. This seems to me the best position for its advocates to adopt.

As to the *a priori* answer, while there may be philosophers who use the word " philosophical " in the way this answer would imply, there must surely be others who do not. The chief point of interest is to know whether there are good reasons for adopting the outlook expressed by one manner of using the word rather than that expressed by the other.

The inductive answer cannot as yet be given in a manner satisfactory to all philosophers. Language-minded philosophers have given solutions of a series of Problems which if accepted would constitute good grounds for Verbalism. But almost every step in the inductive proof is disputable. To prove Verbalism, its advocates need to prove their solutions of each individual Problem.

To put the point more generally, any proposition to the effect that all philosophical Problems have a certain character itself expresses a philosophy. To attempt to prove Verbalism, or any similar generalisation, is to try to convert all philosophers to a single outlook. No doubt it is proper to make the attempt. But I suspect that the piecemeal method is the most promising. In making this remark I am myself making a disputable generalisation about the nature of philosophy. But I do not seek to prove it.

(7)

There are various matters of detail in Hampshire's paper which I find obscure or doubtful. Here I shall refer to two of them.

I do not find it easy to follow Hampshire's discussion, in his third section, of " comparisons between languages or kinds of languages ". He discusses a procedure of " prescribing rules for the translation of those sentences in our ordinary language which would ordinarily be said to describe states of mind " into sentences of a " behaviourist language ". The impression given is that by applying the rules in question we shall be able to associate such a sentence as " he is happy " with such a sentence as " he is disposed to smile ", and that in doing so we shall be giving a sentence in one language as a translation of a sentence in the other.

But a little later Hampshire speaks of a process of "drawing attention to the differences in the use of ... the word 'emotion' in a behaviourist language and in ordinary language". This is puzzling, because on the interpretation I have just given such words as "emotion" will not occur in a behaviourist language. It looks as though we are concerned, not with two "languages", but with two interpretations of a single language.

I am not happy about Hampshire's discussion of the distinction between questions of fact and questions of language (section 4 and elsewhere). I think he is too respectful to this distinction. I can only deal with the point summarily.

Let $A(Q)$ be an analytic proposition, the answer to an essentially Verbal Question, Q. When we call Q a question of language, we are referring to the fact that $A(Q)$ is Validated by $A(Q_L)$. If there is no reference to Q_L, neither is there any reference to language. Q_L is a question of language in the sense that it is Linguistic, and it is also a question of fact. Thus we can find (1) non-Linguistic Questions which are not questions of fact; and (2) Linguistic Questions which are questions of fact. Questions of class (1) may be called questions of language if it is held that Questions of class (2) need to be raised in answering them; but in that case questions of fact are being raised in answering them. The only kind of Question I can think of which might be called a question of language but not of fact is the kind of Question whose answer is not a proposition at all, like "what name shall I give my book?"

I suspect that the distinction, though it may serve some purpose in common speech, is of little use to us if we wish to be precise.

(8)

I accept Hampshire's conjecture that the preoccupation with language shown by contemporary philosophers may be transient, and may be connected with a primitive phase in the scientific study of languages. There was a time when philosophers discussed questions which are now dealt with by specialists in physics or psychology : and it may be that a time will come when Problems which it now seems proper for philosophers to discuss will be dealt with by philological specialists. For my part I have no fear that, should such a time come, philosophers will find themselves without an occupation.

III.—By S. Körner.

The problems with which we are here concerned fall, broadly speaking, into two groups. (I) The dispute may, on the one hand, be about (1) the most appropriate title for a list of relationships, which are themselves not controversial, between philosophical propositions, linguistic rules and linguistic behaviour ; (2) the best method of arriving at answers to philosophical problems ; or (3) the best way of formulating philosophical problems and their solutions. (II) It may, on the other hand, concern controversial relations between philosophical propositions, linguistic rules and linguistic behaviour.

Mr. Hampshire and Mr. Duncan-Jones have dealt with both groups of problems. I have no serious objection to raise against what they have said and shall, therefore, attempt to supplement their papers. This seems especially desirable in relation to those kinds of regulative propositions which are being put forward by philosophers as answers to philosophical problems.

I agree with Mr. Hampshire that the phrases " philosophical question ", " question of language " and by implication, " meaningful question ", do not have a firmly established usage. They will be regarded as sign-posts pointing towards a group of problems and different senses of these words will be considered in the course of the argument. My main reason for not adopting the definitions proposed by Mr. Duncan-Jones is that the term " Variant ", which is most important for his argument, is defined too vaguely. Moreover, his definition of " Question of Language " seems to me too wide. If we accepted it, then the question " Has the thing called ' a ' in fact the property called ' P ' ? ", would be a Question of language, even when there is no doubt that the thing is called " a " and the property is called " P ". It is because of this definition that Mr. Duncan-Jones can prove that, in some odd sense, all Problems are Problems of language.

I.

(1) *Linguistic and antilinguistic views as titles of a list of relationships.*—There is at least one issue, on which both those who assert and those who deny that, in any sense of the words, all questions of philosophy are questions of language, seem to disagree. It is the question whether there are synthetic *a priori* propositions. Assuming, as both parties usually do, that meaningful propositions are either empirical propositions or entailments (i.e., propositions asserting or denying the incidence of the relation of entailment), the question is whether there are synthetic entailments. Although this is only part of the question of the symposium, it may serve to illustrate one aspect of the controversy.

Those who deny that there are synthetic entailments seem to argue as follows. In considering any entailment, we cannot find any consistent set of empirical propositions which would not be consistent with it. Therefore, there are no synthetic entailments. The defenders of the view that there are synthetic entailments would not dispute this relationship between entailments and empirical propositions, or (to use a different terminology), between necessary, meaningful sentences and empirical, meaningful sentences. But they would not regard it as a sufficient reason for denying that there are synthetic entailments. They in turn might point out that, e.g., the entailment which asserts the transitivity of the entailment relation is not, in a sufficiently strong sense, logically equivalent to a proposition that a conjunction entails one of its members. Again, their opponents would not dispute the relationship between the two entailments, but they would not regard it as justifying the view that some entailments are synthetic.

Thus both parties might go on writing together a philosophical chapter on the relations between different kinds of entailments, different kinds of empirical propositions and on the relation between empirical propositions and entailments, agreeing about the content of the chapter but disagreeing as to whether its title should be, " There are synthetic entailments " or " There are no synthetic entailments."

What applies here also applies to the larger question as to whether all philosophical questions are questions of language. For here too relationships between different kinds of propositions (or meaningful sentences) are relevant to the answer. These relationships are often not controversial and the dispute concerns the question of which title is less misleading. This is an empirical question largely dependent on the type of person who is to be misled or protected from being misled.

(2) *A controversy about method.*—To ask whether a given problem is a problem of a certain kind may be a mere question of classification which will in no way help towards a solution of the problem. But this need not be so. It may be that by " problems of a certain kind " we mean problems which are to be tackled in one manner rather than in another. Thus the question whether all philosophical questions are questions of language has often been treated as the question whether all philosophical questions should be dealt with in a " linguistic " or some other way. This is mainly a matter of regulative propositions and the dispute concerns their adequacy ; or rather, the comparative adequacy of different sets of regulative propositions.

In order to decide the question we have to ask : What are the regulative propositions which are characteristic of the linguistic method ? We may of course know how to deal with philosophical questions without knowing the regulative propositions which are satisfied by our doing so. (I have throughout tried to keep in mind the distinction between " knowing how " and " knowing that ". Its importance has been shown by Professor Ryle.[1] But in order to evaluate the method we should be greatly helped by making them explicit. We must further ask what we mean by saying that all philosophical problems should be and are best tackled in accordance with these regulative propositions.

One must be careful not to prejudge these questions by definitions. If, *e.g.*, somebody puts forward the regulative proposition that all philosophical questions are questions

---

[1] G. Ryle. " Knowing how and knowing that." *Proceedings of the Aristotelian Society*, 1945-46.

which are to be answered in terms of formation and transformation rules for uninterpreted sentences, then he must not define philosophical questions as questions to which answers can be given in terms of these rules.

There is not, as has been pointed out by Mr. Hampshire, one set of regulative propositions which is accepted as characteristic of the linguistic approach to philosophy, either by all those who advocate such an approach or by all those who deny its appropriateness. To say that the linguistic approach consists in considerations of the use of symbols, without indicating the kinds of use considered, is saying too little. A linguistic approach must be characterized by specific regulative propositions. Carnap's earlier view that philosophy is logical syntax and his later view that it is semiotical analysis.[2] can be regarded as suggestions that certain specific regulative propositions should be satisfied by those who try to solve philosophical problems, combined with the assertion that the conjunction of these regulative propositions is more adequate than any other set of regulative propositions.

Now the adequacy of rules for the solution of problems must be defined with the help of some reference to problems adequately solved according to these rules. Let us assume that we know in general when a philosophical problem is adequately solved. We can then compare the success of a set of " linguistic " regulative propositions with that of one or more sets of " non-linguistic " regulative propositions. Let us further assume that all philosophical problems which have been solved in any other manner can also be solved in the linguistic way. (A philosopher who held a linguistic view might refer to Kant's refutation of the ontological argument as a case in point.) We still cannot, however, answer the question of the symposium regarded as a methodological question, since it would require a comparison between the success of the linguistic and every other approach, whether we know it or not. This would apply not only to solved philosophical problems, but also to unsolved problems and problems as yet unknown. Thus I agree with Mr. Duncan-Jones that the approach which he calls

---

[2] R. Carnap "Introduction to Semantics", (*Harvard Univ. Press*), 1946.

"Verbalism", like every other linguistic approach, can at best be proclaimed as an expression of faith or hope.

But perhaps the dispute really concerns only the question whether a linguistic approach is a fruitful one. This question can be decided by reference to solved problems and here there seems little doubt that the answer should be affirmative.

(3) *A controversy about the formulation of philosophical questions and answers.*—Those who say, *e.g.*, that no empirical proposition is inconsistent with any necessary proposition are often accused of introducing mysterious entities called "propositions". But, it is quickly added, that what they say in this way is not wholly unsound, for it can be expressed without the use of this misleading word, in terms of "meaningful sentences", or in terms of "facts", or some other terms. The merit of the elimination of "proposition" by means of contextual definitions is alleged to consist in making it impossible to deduce that there are propositions. But that there are propositions is often not deduced by the person who asserts relations between propositions. It is deduced for him by those who object to his terminology and would prefer him to express what he wishes to express, *e.g.*, in terms of meaningful sentences instead. He may, of course, retaliate by deducing from his opponent's assertions of relationships between meaningful sentences that there are meanings. But this would not help to clarify the issue.

Let us consider among the many terminologies in which philosophers express non-empirical relationships only two which are at present much in use; a "word-sentence-meaningful" terminology and a "proposition-concept" terminology. I shall use the word "expression" in the sense of "expressum", *i.e.*, as designating what is expressed. We may call expressions (expressa) which can be formulated in both terminologies "neutral expressions" and expressions which can be formulated only in one of them "terminological expressions". Terminological expressions, such as the expression that there are propositions, are neither empirical nor logically necessary. In the second part of this paper only neutral expressions will occur, which will be formulated in a "proposition-concept" terminology and which can in obvious ways also be formulated in a "word-sentence-meaningful" terminology.

Now those who hold linguistic views often argue for a "word-sentence-meaningful" terminology, *i.e.*, for expressing all neutral expressions in this terminology and for rejecting terminological expressions in any other terminology, especially in the "concept-proposition" terminology. They usually argue, firstly, that these terminological expressions are misleading. This is an empirical argument, dependent on those who are alleged to be misled. They argue further that terminological expressions in a "concept-proposition" terminology are meaningless being neither empirical, nor logically necessary. But this argument is based on a definition of "meaningless" which excludes rules as meaningless.

It seems to me that, *e.g.*, "There are propositions" functions as a rule to the effect that neutral expressions should be formulated in a "proposition-concept" terminology; and that "There are no propositions" functions as a rule to the effect that neutral expressions should not be so formulated.

In this connection one may refer to a related controversy concerning the question whether there are properties and relations. Quine and Goodman regard their view that there are no properties (and other abstract entities) as fundamentally based on a philosophical intuition and make an attempt to vindicate this view, which is neither empirical nor logically necessary, by the construction of a calculus.[3] Their self-imposed task could be described as formulating in a "no-property" terminology expressions, which are neutral with respect to a "property" and to a "no-property" terminology.

Terminological expressions or, as we may also call them, terminological rules are often put forward as answers to philosophical questions. They should be distinguished from, or at least regarded as, a subclass of the above-mentioned regulative propositions as to how philosophical problems should be tackled. They should also be distinguished from

---

[3]. Nelson Goodman and W. V. Quine "Steps toward a Constructive Nominalism." *Journal of Symbolic Logic*, 1947.

rules to the effect that certain empirical concepts should be accepted (see below II(4)). Philosophers are concerned with all three kinds of rules which are distinguished by the sort of evidence, in a wide sense of the word, which can be adduced in their support.

Terminological rules, *i.e.*, rules that expressions, which are neutral with respect to a number of terminologies, should be formulated in one of them, are mainly supported by the argument that people will not be misled by accepting them or that they are in greater danger of being misled by accepting other terminological rules. The evidence for rules to the effect that philosophical problems should be tackled in a certain way, consists in the fact that such problems have been solved in accordance with these rules. Rules to the effect that certain empirical concepts are to be accepted, are as will be seen, supported by reference to empirical theories in which these concepts occur.

I agree with Mr. Hampshire that philosophers are frequently concerned with choosing among different sets of rules and that it is logically possible for them to choose any of the alternatives which they are considering. I further agree that empirical propositions are relevant to the choice. I think, however, that Mr. Hampshire pays too much attention to arguments that these rules are, or are not, misleading and does not sufficiently consider the sense, to be discussed below, in which empirical theories are evidence for some regulative, philosophical propositions.

To sum up the contents of this section : As a question concerning the title of a list of agreed relationships, the question of the symposium cannot in general be answered. The appropriate answer depends on the type of person to whom it is addressed. As a question about method it cannot be answered with any certainty, since the correct answer depends on the solution of unsolved and even unknown problems. As a question concerning the choice of terminological rules, the answer again depends on the sort of person to whom it is addressed. There are philosophical questions which are not answered by terminological rules.

II.

(1) *Propositions and meaningful sentences.*—In considering some relations between philosophical propositions, linguistic rules and linguistic behaviour I shall use a " proposition-concept " terminology. Some explanations are given which will enable those who prefer a " word-sentence-meaningful " terminology to express in that terminology what I shall formulate in terms of propositions and concepts.

There are meaningful and meaningless sentences. To say that a sentence is meaningful and to say that it expresses a proposition is to say the same thing. To say that two sentences have the same meaning is to say that they express the same proposition. We could also define a proposition, in a different manner, as a class of sentences with the same meaning, but not as a class of sentences without reference to the meaning of any member of the class. We may know that all sentences of a class have the same meaning without knowing the meaning of any of them.

It is not strictly correct to say that we know the meaning of a sentence if, and only if, we know how to use it in all respects. For knowing how to use it in some respects may be irrelevant to knowing its meaning. Thus, in many cases, knowing how to apply rules of intonation and pronunciation is irrelevant to knowing the meaning of sentences. On the other hand, knowing how to use transformation rules, which does not entail being aware of these rules themselves, is relevant to but not sufficient for knowing the meaning of property—and relation words.

To know the meaning of the sentence " this is a dog " entails knowing the proposition *this is a dog*. We may know this proposition without altogether knowing how to use English words. Those who prefer a linguistic terminology would assert that knowing how to use " this is a dog " or " Das ist ein Hund " or . . . entails and is entailed by knowing the proposition *this is a dog*. To talk about this proposition is then a way of talking about meaningful sentences. I should prefer to use " proposition " in such a way that knowing how to use any of the mentioned sentences entails knowing the proposition *this is a dog* ; but that the converse entailment does not hold. This would leave open as an empirical question, whether knowing a proposition entails knowing how to use a sentence expressing it.

Knowing how to use the meaningful sentence "this is a dog" and the meaningful words "a dog" in inference, entails knowing entailment propositions or entailments, *e.g.*, the entailment that x *is a dog* entails x *is an animal*, whatever x may be. We shall say that this entailment determines the concept x *is a dog*. Knowing an entailment is an empirical fact. So is knowing an empirical proposition. But no entailment entails any empirical proposition.

In entailment propositions the relation of entailment relates two propositions or two concepts (*e.g.*, *this is a dog* and *this is an animal*, or x *is a dog* and x *is an animal*). The propositions thus related may, or may not, themselves be entailments. In the latter case we may call them for the moment "non-entailments". Empirical propositions are a kind of non-entailments. They are characterized by different philosophers in slightly different ways. These differences do not matter here. Propositions that words are being used in certain ways, are empirical.

Rules are different from empirical propositions and from entailments. Rules are satisfied by some actual, or supposed, states of affairs. We shall say of a rule which is satisfied by an actual, or supposed, state of affairs, that it is also satisfied by the empirical proposition which corresponds to this state of affairs. The relation expressed by "is satisfied", does not hold between any two empirical propositions, or between any entailment and any empirical proposition.

(2) *A sense in which entailments are based on rules and empirical propositions.*—Whether, or not, all questions of philosophy are questions of language is mainly discussed with regard to those philosophical questions, to which the answers are entailments or necessary propositions. The reason for this consists in the assumption made by both parties that only empirical propositions and entailments are meaningful.

If some philosophical questions are answered by entailments, then the question of the symposium requires us to consider the relation between entailments, on the one hand,

and linguistic rules and linguistic facts, on the other. Mr. Hampshire seems to assume that those philosophical questions, which are answered by entailments are, in an acceptable sense, which need not be explained further, questions of language. Mr. Duncan-Jones also does not inquire into the relation between linguistic facts and necessary propositions.

Entailments, or necessary propositions, have been regarded as being variously a special kind of rules, a special kind of empirical propositions, or as being " based upon " such propositions. If this last assertion, or Mr. Duncan-Jones' reference to " a strange and interesting kind of deducibility ", which he calls " validation ", is intended to mean no more than that entailments, empirical, especially linguistic propositions, and rules, especially linguistic rules, are related in some close manner, it can be shown to be correct.

We shall first consider some relationships between non-linguistic rules, non-linguistic empirical propositions and entailments. Let us take as an example the rule to the effect that I should do some exercise in the morning (r) and the empirical proposition that I am riding a bicycle in the morning(s). Ovbiously r is satisfied by other propositions besides s, which may be inconsistent with each other. Among all these propositions there is one which is entailed by any of them. It can be expressed by saying that I am doing some exercise in the morning. We may call it the indicative of r and write " s " for it. With every rule there is given the class of all empirical propositions which satisfy it and also its indicative. Now, the propositions that s satisfies r and that s entails s_n entail each other and there is thus a class of cases where an entailment is logically equivalent to the proposition that an empirical proposition (or, if we like, a state of affairs, or behaviour) satisfies a rule.

But I suspect that this would not satisfy most of those who hold that entailments are based on rules or empirical propositions. They wish to show that empirical propositions as such, or rules as such, give rise, in some special compulsory manner, to necessary propositions.

It seems that sometimes the impression that rules as such, or empirical propositions as such, " unavoidably give rise to ", but do not entail, entailments is due to a confusion between empirical propositions *which* satisfy certain rules, or rules *which* are satisfied by empirical propositions, on the one hand, and propositions *that* certain rules are satisfied by empirical propositions, on the other. But rules, which ....., are still rules and empirical propositions, which ....., are still empirical propositions. By confusing the empirical proposition p, which satisfies certain rules, on the one hand, with the non-empirical proposition that p satisfies these rules, on the other, one might be led to believe that p gives rise in some peculiar manner to the necessary proposition to which the proposition that p satisfies these rules is logically equivalent. A similar confusion between the rule which is satisfied by p and the proposition that the rule is satisfied by p, may have led others to believe that rules give rise in some peculiar way to necessary propositions.

We must now consider relations between empirical propositions about linguistic behaviour, linguistic rules and necessary propositions. Propositions describing linguistic behaviour are empirical. Rules satisfied by such propositions are linguistic rules. To consider that somebody's linguistic behaviour is correct with regard to certain rules, is to consider that a certain state of affairs (and the empirical proposition corresponding to it) satisfies these rules. Similarly, to assert that a string of symbols is a sentence of a certain language, or that a sentence is correctly derived according to the rules of this language, is not to assert an empirical proposition, but that certain states of affairs satisfy certain rules.

One may be mistaken as to whether a string of symbols is a sentence, or whether a sentence is correctly derived. But such a mistake is like believing that a certain proposition is entailed by a proposition by which it is not entailed, or that it is not entailed by a proposition by which it is entailed. This follows from the logical enquivalence of the proposition that p satisfies the rule r with the proposition that p entails the indicative of r.

Manipulating a fixed number of signs according to fixed rules of formation and transformation is manipulating an uninterpreted calculus. It was believed at one time that in some way, or other, manipulating symbols, which symbolized nothing, according to rules of formation and transformation, " gave rise " to necessary propositions other than those which are equivalent to propositions that certain manipulations or their results satisfy these rules. But now many philosophers, who inclined to this view assume that manipulating a calculus is not enough. They now hold that such manipulation, together with the assignment of meaning to the symbols which are manipulated, gives rise to necessary propositions, or entailments.

Professor Ayer in his preface to the second edition of " Language, Truth and Logic " (p. 17), gives the following example : " Thus, it is a contingent, empirical fact that the word " earlier " is used in English to mean earlier, and it is an arbitrary, though convenient, rule of language that words that stand for temporal relations are to be used transitively ; but, given this rule, the proposition that, if A is earlier than B and B is earlier than C, A is earlier than C becomes a necessary truth ". In other words, because of the empirical fact that people manipulate " earlier " in accordance with certain rules and, because of the further empirical fact that to them " earlier " means earlier, a certain sentence expresses a necessary proposition. But that a sentence expresses a necessary proposition is itself an empirical proposition which is entailed by other empirical propositions about the use and the meaning of words. It seems, therefore, that the relation designated by " based on ", which relates linguistic facts and necessary propositions, can be analysed in terms of entailment between empirical propositions. What is entailed by empirical propositions about the use of words is not a necessary proposition (an entailment), but the empirical proposition that a certain sentence expresses a necessary proposition. It is difficult to see what else could be meant by those who assert that necessary propositions are " based on " linguistic facts.

(3) *On accepting and rejecting entailments and concepts.*—Knowing the meaning of a property-, or relation-word, entails knowing how to use it in inference; and this entails knowing entailments and the concepts determined by them. My knowing entailments does not entail my actually applying

to anything the concepts which are determined by them. For instance, if I know how to use the words " a dog " in inference, then I necessarily know, *e.g.*, the entailment that *x is a dog* entails *x is an animal*. But this knowledge does not entail my ever actually applying the concept *x is a dog* by asserting, or denying of any particular being, that it is a dog in English, or in any other language.

In the same way that knowing entailments and the concepts determined by them are empirical facts, so applying and being inclined to apply them are also empirical facts. Instead of, " knowing entailments and applying, or being inclined to apply, the concept which is determined by them", we shall say, " accepting entailments and the concept determined by them ". If we know a concept, or entailment, and do not accept it, we may be said to reject it.

The acceptance and rejection of concepts and thereby of entailments by which these concepts are determined, are empirical facts. Conceptual systems may become and do, in fact, become obsolete. We may know the concepts expressed by some Greek words and yet not accept them. There are different kinds of entailments, acceptance, or rejection, of which shows important differences relevant to the question of the symposium. In some entailments, the relation of entailment relates propositions which are themselves not entailments. That *x is a dog* entails *x is an animal* would be an example. It is in the case of such entailments and of the concepts determined by them, that we are familiar with their acceptance or rejection. We are told, for instance, that the concept of mechanical causation had been accepted for a long time by almost all physicists and is now rejected by most of them.

In other entailments the relation of entailment relates entailment propositions. Knowing how to use the word " entails " meaningfully entails knowing such entailments, whether they are expressed in words of the English language, or any other language. An example of such a proposition could be expressed by the sentence " (p entails q) and (q entails r) entail (p entails r) ". It is conceivable that such entailments should be rejected. But their rejection would be the rejection of the concept of entailment which is determined by them and in the application of which inference consists. Whatever " thinking " may mean, inference is included in thinking and a person who decides to reject these entailments decides to stop thinking.

We must now ask again whether all questions to which the answers are entailments are questions of language. From the above mentioned relationships and differences between various kinds of propositions there follows neither an affirmative, nor a negative, answer. It is also not clear whether, in order not to mislead anybody, including oneself, one should not head the list of these relationships in one way or another. It might for instance seem to some that the logical equivalence of propositions such as *p satisfies r* to entailments, points to a positive answer. They might see a further justification for such an answer in the fact that we frequently accept and reject entailments which do not themselves relate entailments. They may even, in spite of agreeing with our account of the relation designated by the words " based on ", see in this relationship some support for an affirmative answer. On the other hand, a negative answer may seem less misleading, if one considers that entailments neither entail, nor are entailed by, empirical propositions ; and that the decision to reject entailments which relate entailments, is a decision to stop thinking. But while it is important to be clear about these and many other relationships, it is much less important to decide on a general title for them.

(4) *Regulative propositions to the effect that certain empirical concepts should be accepted.*—Mr. Hampshire and Mr. Duncan-Jones consider only entailments and empirical propositions as meaningful. I believe that such a definition of " meaningfulness " is inconveniently narrow and not in accordance with ordinary usage. If one were looking for a definition of " meaningful propositions " which would not be purely enumerative, one would, in any case, require that empirical propositions should fall under it. Of all other propositions, one would require some sufficiently intimate relation to empirical propositions. This vague requirement would be regarded as fulfilled by entailments. Those who regard metaphysical propositions as meaningful would claim that

the connection between empirical propositions and metaphysical propositions lies in the fact that both kinds of propositions are, although in different ways, about the world or reality. Metaphysical philosophers often adduce the results of empirical investigations as evidence for empirical propositions.

It is, I believe, generally recognized that experiments and observations are evidence for scientific theories in a sense of " evidence " which is different from the sense in which empirical propositions and scientific theories could be said, if at all, to be " evidence for " metaphysical propositions. To make matters less obscure, a relation between empirical and metaphysical propositions would have to be shown such that, in some cases at least, preferring one set of empirical propositions to another, commits us to preferring one set of metaphysical propositions to another.

It is possible to regard some metaphysical propositions as regulative propositions to the effect that certain empirical concepts should be accepted rather than others. (An empirical concept is a concept whose incidence is asserted by an empirical proposition). Thus to use an example given earlier : A philosophy of Mechanism may be regarded as consisting of directions to the effect that, among other concepts, a concept of mechanical causation should be accepted. From Mechanism we distinguish other sets of metaphysical, regulative propositions. We may call one of them Antimechanism. Let us now assume that accepting the concepts occurring in certain empirical theories satisfies Mechanism, and that accepting the concepts occurring in other empirical theories satisfies Antimechanism. Let us further assume that both sets of empirical theories can be compared with regard to their adequacy and that " adequacy " is not defined by reference to the regulative propositions of either Mechanism, or Antimechanism. Then we could regard the more adequate set of empirical theories as a kind of evidence for that set of regulative propositions which is satisfied by the acceptance of the concepts which occur in these theories. I am here not concerned with elaborating and defending this view. It may lead us to regard regulative metaphysical propositions of the kind described, as standing in a sufficiently close relation to empirical propositions as to be included among meaningful propositions.

But, if these metaphysical propositions are meaningful answers to philosophical questions, are they at the same time answers to questions of language? Before again refusing to give a definite answer, a distinction must be made. A philosopher may regard it as his task to make explicit the regulative propositions which are satisfied by given empirical theories. He may also regard it as his task to suggest regulative propositions which are not satisfied by any given empirical theory; or, as, I believe, happens more frequently, to suggest regulative propositions, which are satisfied by some empirical theories only. He may, in other words, not only lay bare regulative propositions which are satisfied by some scientific theories and other sets of empirical propositions, but also suggest the reconstruction of other theories in accordance with these regulative propositions.

If he only makes explicit the regulative propositions which are satisfied by certain empirical theories, he draws attention to a kind of propositions which we have considered above, namely, to propositions that rules are satisfied by states of affairs, or empirical propositions. These propositions are logically equivalent to entailments. Consequently, what has been said about entailments, could similarly be said about these propositions.

The case is different if a philosopher puts forward regulative propositions, for which some empirical theories are " evidence ", together with the suggestion that other empirical theories should be reconstructed in accordance with these regulative propositions. If he puts forward, *e.g.*, mechanistic principles in this manner, then he must be said to be answering philosophical questions, if we wish to call " philosophical " an activity which is characteristic of most philosophers. He cannot be described as also answering a question of language, unless at the same time attention is drawn to the great difference between the use of the word " language " in this context and its other uses. Some of the latter have been discussed by Mr. Hampshire and by Mr. Duncan-Jones.

THE EMOTIVE THEORY OF ETHICS

Mr. Richard Robinson, Prof. H. J. Paton and
Mr. R. C. Cross.

I.—*By* Richard Robinson.

What shall we mean by " the emotive theory of ethics " ? It must be some theory which implies that there is such a thing as independent emotive meaning as described in Professor Stevenson's *Ethics and Language*. Emotive meaning is the power of a word to express and arouse feeling, as opposed to its power to express and arouse the thought of an object. A word may describe or name an object : that is its descriptive function. A word may arouse a feeling ; that is its emotive function. A word may arouse a feeling simply because it names some object and the thought of that object arouses the feeling ; that is dependent emotive meaning. But " the emotive theory of ethics " must mean some theory which implies that a word may also have independent emotive meaning. Independent emotive meaning is the power of a word to arouse emotion independently of what it describes or names. The best way of demonstrating its occurrence would be to find a pair of words which name the same thing but arouse different feelings towards it ; for, if there is such a pair, the power of at least one of the pair to arouse emotion must be at least partly independent of its power to arouse the thought of that thing. Perhaps you will agree that the following list contains at least one pair of words that name the same thing but arouse different emotions towards it :

> to ape—to imitate
> nigger—negro
> murder—slaughter—liquidate—kill—execute
> liberty—license
> penalize—punish
> lust—sexual desire.

Another argument in favour of the occurrence of independent emotive meaning is to urge that some interjections have an emotive meaning which must be independent of their descriptive meaning because they have no descriptive meaning. Thus it may be said that the words " alas " and " ouch " and " ugh," which certainly express emotion, do not describe at all. For example, to utter " alas " is not, even in part, to state that one feels sad or that something is saddening, or to state anything.

This first determination of what we are to mean by " the emotive theory of ethics " is already sufficient to make some people reject the theory; for I have known at least one thinker who held that independent emotive meaning never occurs. I am unable, however, to report his reason, or any reason for that view. To me it seems, as it did to Berkeley (*Principles*, Introduction, No. 20), an obvious fact of experience that independent emotive meaning occurs.

(2) Under the name of " the emotive theory of ethics " we must further include the view that ethical words have independent emotive meaning. We cannot give a complete list of ethical words, or find an easy method of determining whether any given word is ethical; but all we need to do here is to list a few of them. Ethical words include " good," " bad," " evil," " right," " wrong," " ought," " duty," " obligation," " sin," many senses of " can " and " cannot " and " must " and " may," " proper," " improper," " admirable," " contemptible," " just," " unjust," " fair," " unfair," " shocking," " guilty," " responsible." I should like if I may, to include also under " ethical words " the aesthetic words, such as " beautiful," " ugly," " lovely," " charming." But, if you find this an unnatural stretching of the word " ethics," I could speak of " the emotive theory of axiology " instead of " the emotive theory of ethics," and bring in the aesthetic words in that way. We certainly want to mean by " the emotive theory of ethics (or axiology)" some view according to which each of these words produces an emotional effect independently of naming or describing any object it may name.

This second specification causes a further group of persons to reject the emotive theory of ethics, a very large group this time. For, while everybody admits that an ethical word has the power to arouse feelings, a great many people deny that this power is independent of the descriptive function of the word. They hold that the word " good," for example, involves no emotion of approval or esteem directly, but only indirectly through evoking the thought of the attribute goodness, whose name it is. According to them it is the attribute goodness, not the word " good," that evokes the emotion in us. According to Sir David Ross in *The Foundations of Ethics*, for example, the word " good " could not evoke an emotion of approval apart from evoking the idea of goodness because " it is impossible to approve of anything without thinking it *worthy* of approval—without thinking that it has a goodness of its own which makes it fit to be approved. . . If things were only approved, without anything being worthy of approval, the act of approval would simply be nonsensical " (*FE* 261—2).

I find this contention of Sir David's unpersuasive. What sort of impossibility has he in mind ? Casual impossibility, I suppose ; for he must be talking about the laws of psychology. He seems to be saying that it is a law of human nature that, whenever a human being approves of anything, he always without exception thinks that that thing has a goodness of its own which makes it fit to be approved. If this is the meaning, I can only report that I am strongly inclined to disbelieve it ; and that I rather wonder that Sir David is willing to commit himself to the assertion of a one-hundred-per-cent. correlation in a matter of psychology. Is it safe in psychology to commit oneself to more than statements of tendency and statements of occurrence : " A tends to be accompanied by B " ; and " A sometimes is accompanied by B " ; but not " A always is accompanied by B " ?

In the second sentence which I have quoted Sir David appeals not to impossibility but to nonsensicality. " If things were only approved, without anything being worthy of approval, the act of approval would simply be nonsensical."

A nonsensical act is the same thing, I suppose, as a very silly or pointless act. Here again I disagree with Sir David ; I do not judge it silly to approve of something without thinking that it possesses the attribute goodness. Anyhow, from the premiss that a certain type of act is very silly it by no means follows that that type of act never occurs.

The confidence, with which Sir David here asserts an invariable connexion between approving x and thinking that x has the attribute goodness, seems more appropriate to the enunciation of a tautology than of a psychological generalisation. And there is a certain tautology that comes to mind at this point. For there are emotive tautologies as well as descriptive tautologies. It is tautologous to say that x is x, whether the function of the word " x " here is descriptive or emotive. It is tautologous to say that we ought not to do wrong, because " ought not " and " wrong " are two emotive terms that arouse much the same emotion. The statement " I approve of x," while it has a clear descriptive function, also has an emotive function which is much the same as the emotive functions of the sentences " x is good " and " x is worthy of approval." Therefore, to say " I approve of x " is in part to do the same thing as when we say " x is good " or " x is worthy of approval."

This argument is the only argument in the whole of *The Right and the Good* and *The Foundations of Ethics* which makes against the emotive theory of ethics as so far stated. Nearly all the arguments in those books are directed against certain theories about the *descriptive* functions of ethical words, not about their *emotive* functions. For example, the theory that when we say " x is good " we are *describing* somebody's approval of x, as opposed to the theory that when we say " x is good " we are *evoking* somebody's approval of x. Sir David spends many pages rebutting theories to the effect that " x is good " is a *description* of some attitude, and only one page rebutting the theory that " x is good" is an *evocation* of some attitude. This distribution of labour seems unsuitable in view of the fact that he thinks the latter view more plausible than the former. He writes : " The most plausible form in which the relational view could be expressed would be to say that nothing possesses the kind of intrinsic characteristic which we ascribe to things when we call them good ; that some things are, however, actual or possible objects of a favourable emotion, and that on the strength of this we mistakenly ascribe to them goodness in themselves." (*FE* 261). He then proceeds to rebut this " most plausible form of the relational view " in one page, after having taken 3 pages in this book, and 30 in the earlier book, to rebut the less plausible form.

(3) Let us now take a third step in defining what we propose to mean by " the emotive theory of ethics." It seems that the emotive theory of ethics cannot confine itself to talking about the emotive functions of ethical terms, as we have done so far, but must also say something about their descriptive functions. It will say something sceptical about the descriptive functions of ethical terms as commonly understood. For, if it left standing all that, for example, Sir David Ross says about the descriptive functions of " good " and " right " in *The Right and the Good*, it would not have anything of the flavour that we all ascribe to it.

At this point the theory might take many different forms. I shall bring forward only one of them, the one that seems most likely to me now. In this form I complete the definition of " the emotive theory of ethics " by adding to the two propositions already obtained the following two :—

> 3. The descriptive function of the ethical words is more or less as elucidated by Sir David Ross in *The Right and the Good*. That is to say, they name unanalysable qualities belonging to certain acts or objects in complete independence of all human feelings and thoughts.

>   4. In this descriptive use the ethical words involve an error, because nothing has such an unanalysable independent attribute as they name.

With regard to the third proposition, one of the great benefits which *The Right and the Good* has given us is the clear and emphatic revelation of the pervasive tendency of ethical words to exercise a descriptive function consisting in naming an independent unanalysable attribute. When the question is what we actually mean, in common speech, by the words " right " and " good " and " beautiful," then, as far as their descriptive function is concerned, Sir David Ross seems to me to have given the clearest statement of the true answer.

There is, however, one respect in which I should like to alter Sir David's account. I should like him to admit more vagueness and shiftingness in the descriptive work of the ethical terms as commonly used. His language from time to time gives the impression that, if we analyse carefully enough, we shall eventually discover *precisely* what the ethical terms mean. I think, following Professor Stevenson, that we shall never do this because the ethical terms in common usage do not mean *precisely* anything, any more than the term " yellow " in common usage indicates precisely where yellow becomes orange. Any precision that there might be in the descriptive use of the ethical words would be the result of deliberate introduction by arbitrary definition. It would alter what we really mean by these words in common usage; and we should find that the alteration had disadvantages as well as advantages. Their use as the names of independent unanalysable qualities is an important and frequent tendency of the ethical words, rather than *precisely* what they mean.

If we stop at the third proposition, the emotive theory of ethics is compatible with ethical objectivism. For by

" ethical objectivism " I mean, I hope, the view that some statements of the forms

> " x is good "
> " x is bad "
> " x is right "
> " x is wrong "
> " x is beautiful "
> " A ought to have done x "
> " A ought not to have done x "

are true descriptions of facts independent of all human feelings. Thus according to ethical objectivism goodness may be either indefinable or definable, but if it is definable the definition includes nothing about human feelings. Thus, also, ethical objectivism is not merely a view about what is commoly meant by the forms " x is good " etc., but also the view that some statements falling under these forms are true, i.e., describe the world as it actually is. We can easily imagine a thinker who says he is an ethical objectivist if we omit the word " true " from our definition ; he would agree that some statements of these forms are meant to describe facts independent of all human feelings ; but he would hold that they all fail to do so because there are no such independent facts as they purport to describe. Such a view is not ethical objectivism by my definition because of the word " true " which I have inserted.

By " ethical subjectivism " I will try to mean the exact contradictory of ethical objectivism. A formulation of this contradictory can be obtained by substituting the word " no " for the word " some " in the above definition of " ethical objectivism." Ethical subjectivism (in this sense of the phrase) is compatible with nine-tenths of what Sir David Ross explicitly wrote in *The Right and the Good*. For the point he was explicitly making there was not that some statements of these forms are *true* descriptions of facts independent of all human feelings, but merely that they are *descriptions* of such facts. He reiterated that he was telling us what we really mean by these forms of words. As to whether what we really mean to say happens to be the truth or not, as to whether we are mistaken or correct in asserting that " x is good" in the sense in which we do assert it—about that very little is explicitly said in *The Right and the Good*, although it is always clear by implication what the author's answer is.

If we confine ourselves to the first three propositions, the emotive theory of ethics is compatible with either objectivism or subjectivism in ethics. It entails subjectivism, however, when we add the fourth proposition, which is that in their descriptive use the ethical words involve an error, because there is no such independent unanalysable attribute as they name.

This form of subjectivism, and of the emotive theory of ethics, according to which there is a pervasive tendency to error in our ordinary ethical language, is not very common in the literature. There is, however, a clear statement of it by John Mackie in *The Australasian Journal of Psychology and Philosophy* XXIV. And it was adopted with regard to one axiological term by Sir David Ross, from whose doctrine I shall start my own account.

In *The Right and the Good* Sir David found that we mean by the word " beautiful " an attribute that has no reference to a mind, " something entirely resident in the object, apart from relation to a mind " (p. 128 n.). And he found the same of the word " good." By each of these words, according to him, we intend an entirely objective attribute, quite independent of all minds.

But Sir David judged the correctness of our usage very differently in the two cases ; for his opinion was that, while we are right to mean by the word " good " an utterly independent attribute, since there is such an attribute, we are wrong and " deceived " in meaning such an independent attribute by the word " beautiful," since beautiful things have no common attribute except the power of producing aesthetic enjoyment, which is relative to minds.

I am glad to have this statement from a first-class philosopher that we can be deceived in our usage of a word, and that we can mean by a word an independent attribute when there is no such attribute in the things to which we apply the word, or anywhere at all. For the fact that a first-class philosopher has said that in using a certain axiological word, namely " beautiful," we are believing in the occurrence of a certain independent attribute which never does occur, must shield me from all accusations of impropriety or folly in suggesting that the same is true of other axiological words. I suggest that we are equally deceived in our use of the word " good " ; that we use it to mean an attribute entirely independent of minds, but there is no such attribute ; that what Sir David said of the word " beautiful " is true also of the word " good." If we analyse Sir David's views here into four parts :—

1. By the word " good " we mean an entirely independent attribute.
2. There is such an attribute.
3. By the word " beautiful " we mean an entirely independent attribute,
4. There is no such attribute ; we are deceived ;

then we can state my suggestion as the suggestion that Sir David's four propositions would all be true if we merely changed the second to read, in perfect symmetry with the fourth: " There is no such an attribute; we are deceived."

The above interpretation of Sir David Ross's book may seem mistaken to those who do not recall the brief passage on which it is based (p. 128 n.) and do recall the longer passage developing the view that beauty is the power of producing aesthetic enjoyment in minds. According to this passage, it may be urged, the word " beauty " must mean something not independent of minds.

It is a fact that Sir David said both that beauty is a certain power relative to minds, and that we mean by the word " beauty " a certain attribute not relative to minds. And this raises a difficulty. For if in the first sentence we substitute for the word " beauty " what we are entitled to substitute by the second sentence, we get the absurd result that " a certain attribute not relative to minds is a certain power relative to minds." The solution of this difficulty seems to be that, when he suggested that beauty is the power of producing aesthetic enjoyment in minds, Sir David was, though he did not say so, recommending us to *alter* our conception of beauty and our use of the word " beauty." His two apparently contradictory doctrines may be combined in the following consistent whole : " We commonly conceive of beauty as an attribute independent of minds, and we commonly use the word " beauty " in accordance with this conception. Since, however, there is no such independent attribute in the things we call beautiful, our conception is an error and our usage involves a mistake. I therefore propose (we must take Sir David as saying) that we alter and improve our conception of beauty, and take it henceforth as the power of producing aesthetic enjoyment, and alter our use of the word " beauty " accordingly ; for in this new form the conception and the word will be useful and correspond to some reality, which they fail to do in their ordinary form."

I suggest in my forthcoming essay on definition, that much of what is offered as the definition or analysis of an attribute is not really the analysis of an attribute but the proposal to think about a slightly different attribute in future, on the ground that our current conception is confused or applies to nothing real. For example, the definition of infinity as the attribute of a set consisting in its being able to be put into one-one correspondence with some of its own subsets, is not really an analysis of the attribute people begin by thinking of under the name " infinity " ; it is a suggestion that they had better think of this new attribute instead, because it is more precise and freer from contradiction. Sir David Ross was suggesting that, since there is no independent attribute belonging to the Mona Lisa such as we commonly imply when we call it " beautiful," we had better change our conception of beauty, and in future, when we call a picture " beautiful," we had better mean that it has the power to arouse the aesthetic pleasure in men.

In a similar way we might suggest that, since there is no independent attribute belonging to virtue such as we commonly imply when we call it " good," we had better change our conception of goodness and mean something else by the word " good."

But what should we choose to mean in future by the word " good " ? Sir David Ross chose to mean by the word " beautiful " the only attribute he could find actually common to all the things called " beautiful," namely their power to cause a single kind of experience. So if we could find that the things called " good " all had power to cause a single kind of experience, we might perhaps make that power our new conception of goodness. Now there is one kind of experience which everybody has from an object when he sincerely and independently calls it " good," namely the experience of approving it or otherwise favourably valuing it. It would be possible, therefore, to mean by the " goodness " of a thing in future its power of evoking favourable evaluation from somebody.

But few people would consent to adopt this usage, for the following reason. Many things, and perhaps all things, have both the power of eliciting approval from somebody and the power of eliciting disapproval from somebody. Consequently, if I decide to call a thing " good " because somebody approves of it, I may find myself obliged to call everything " good," and I may find myself obliged to call " good " many things which I disapprove and wish to prevent. But no one is willing to call a thing " good " if he disapproves it and wishes to prevent it.

Here we have a most important fact about our conception of goodness and our use of the word " goodness." No one is willing to call a thing " good " if he disapproves it and wishes to prevent it. Why is this ? I believe it is because we are all aware that the word " good " has a certain practical force, which we can no more alter by our definitions than most of us can alter the economic system of our country. On the one hand, this practical force is something human and contingent. It belongs not to the mere noise " good," nor to the mere letters on paper, but to these forms as habitually functioning in the minds of men. And they might have functioned in some other way in our minds, or not at all. It is contingent that the Teutonic word " gut " has taken over this function among us, and not the Latin word " bonum." On the other hand, this practical force of the word " good," human and contingent though it is, is quite unalterable by most of us, and comes to nearly every one of us as an inexorable necessity to which he must conform.

The nature of this inevitable practical force is that, each time we declare to another man that x is good, we are doing something that tends to make him approve x or evaluate it favourably. The influence is often extremely slight, like the force of gravity; but, like the force of gravity, it is always there, and one cannot legislate it out of existence. And, further, each time another man declares to us that x is good, he not being ironical or mad or irreconcilably hostile, he influences us to value x favourably, though the influence is often extremely slight and comes to nothing.

This is an example of the remarkable fact that, whereas the descriptive function of words can be altered by deliberate definition, their emotive function cannot be. It is possible to say " let the word ' culture ' mean henceforth in this book familiarity with the products of artists and scientist ", and by this mere fiat to cause the word to function so to one's readers. But to say " let the word ' culture ' henceforth in this book arouse the emotions of pity and fear " is quite ineffective. The emotional force of words is far less amenable to alteration than their descriptive force. The sentence " x is good " insists on tending to arouse approval of x in speaker and hearer, and no legislative definition can prevent it from doing so.

The fact, that you do not remove the emotive force of a word by saying that you are removing, makes it possible to use the emotive force of a word while pretending not to. You declare that the word is not to be understood in what follows as having its usual emotive force; then you use the word; and it does have its usual emotive force. Thus Veblen in his *Theory of the Leisure Class* said the word " waste " was not to be taken as a term of disapproval in that book, and thus pretended not to be pouring scorn on the rich when he went on to say that their characteristic is conspicuous waste. Thus Churchill speculated whether the speaker " would admit the word ' lousy ' as a parliamentary expression in referring to the Administration, provided, of course, it was not intended in a contemptuous sense, but purely as one of factual narration."

Another important characteristic of the emotive dimension of meaning is that there are few or no emotive synonyms and equivalents within a single language. The emotive effect of saying " I ought to do this " cannot be exactly reproduced by saying anything else. It is not exactly the same as the emotional effect of any description, such as " I approve of my doing this," or of any command, such as " let me do this," or of any interjection. It can only be compared to other sentences and said to resemble them in some respects but not in others. We should abandon the search for sentences equivalent to " I ought to do this " or " that is bad " or the like. There probably are none; and if there were, what particular advantage would it be to find them ? Instead, we should try to *characterize* the emotive force of these sentences, to bring out some of their features, using partial comparisons and probably also metaphors. Professor Stevenson has done some excellent work along this line; but most of his readers will overlook that, and take him as suggesting that there is an equivalent to " x is good," namely " I approve of x ; do so as well."

If a word has both an emotional and a descriptive function, that is, if it both evokes an emotion and indicates a thing, the combined effect of these two functions is to direct the emotion towards the thing. The words " to ape " and " to imitate " indicate the same form, and evoke different emotions towards it. The effect of redefining the descriptive function of a word that has a strong emotive function is, as Professor Stevenson has shown us, to redirect the emotional attitude evoked by the word, away from what it formerly described, towards what it describes according to the new definition. Since the word " good " has a strong and ineradicable power to arouse approval, the effect of any definition which gives it a descriptive function is to invite approval of that which, by the definition, it is to describe. The effect of defining goodness as coherence, for example, is to express and invite approval of coherence. This is the reason why few people would be willing to mean by the " goodness " of a thing its power of evoking favourable evaluation from somebody. In using the word so, they would be expressing and encouraging the approval of all powers to evoke approval. But they do not wish to do this. For example, a man who disapproves of compulsion does not wish to express or evoke approval of the power of compulsion to evoke approval from some people. In general, if he disapproves of x, he disapproves of any power that x has to evoke approval ; hence he will not increase x's power to evoke approval ; but he *would* tend to increase it if he called x " good," by the nature of the word " good " ; hence he will not call x " good."

To give a descriptive definition of goodness, to assign a descriptive function to the word " good," is inevitably to take sides in the world in a very practical way. It is to throw your weight—and every sane human inevitably has some weight—in favour of the thing which you make the word " good " describe.

The kind of definition which assigns a descriptive function, or a new descriptive function, to a word which has a strong evaluative function, and thus directs this sort of evaluation towards a specific object, was called by its discoverer " persuasive definition." This phrase, however, is liable to be taken in its more obvious sense, of a definition which people are strongly inclined to believe true ; and I suggest that we substitute the phrase " evaluative definition." The purpose of such a definition is to express and procure the evaluation of the thing specified in the way evoked by the word's emotive function.

When our aim is to know and not to alter, it is essential for us to distinguish the evaluative from the descriptive function and use the latter only. This is very difficult to do when discussing morality and values. If an ethical philosopher suggests that there is no independent attribute goodness such as we commonly mean by the word " good," he intends this to be a purely scientific statement, merely expressing knowledge, and not in any way evaluating the world or intervening in it. But so intense and electric is the practical force of the word " good " that even when handled with the thickest gloves it will still seem to some people to be being used evaluatively, and not merely scientifically described. There are always some people who misinterpret the merely descriptive statement that there is no independent attribute such as is commonly intended by the word " good," and take it to be an evaluative utterance, the expression of a judgment on the world and the invitation to others to judge likewise.

(I do not confine the word "judgment" to acts which are true or false. I include in the " judgment " both the thought that A killed B, which has a truth value, and the evaluation that A should be hanged, which has no truth value. I think this accords with the common usage of the word "judgment." The word " opinion " also seems to refer to an act of evaluating quite as often as to an act of believing.)

What specific form will this misinterpretation take? When the scientific statement that there is no independent attribute goodness is mistaken for an evaluation, what evaluation specifically will it be mistaken for? It will be mistaken for that peculiar evaluation which consists in repudiating all values. It will be supposed to be a confession of indifference to everything, and a refusal to join the hearer in valuing anything he may value. Since indifference is itself a value-attitude, and like all value-attitudes is catching, and since indifference to all values includes indifference to each hearer's most cherished and important values, each mistaken interpreter of the scientific statement will feel in it a danger to his own most urgent values. If, for instance, he intensely values freedom and justice, and intensely desires everyone else to value them intensely too, and sometimes expresses this by the asseveration that freedom and justice are objectively and eternally good, independently of all human valuations, then the scientific statement that there is no independent goodness, misinterpreted as an evaluation, will seem to him to include a refusal to care about freedom and justice and to propagate the habit of caring about them. And this is the cause of the terror and emotion with which some objectivists regard subjectivist theories of goodness. The word " good," like all the very strong evaluative words, is extremely difficult to mention without at the same time using it, or at least seeming to use it to some of one's hearers. And when subjectivist *theories about* the word " good " are mistaken for evaluative *uses of* the word " good," the kind of use they naturally seem to be is a repudiation of all values.

The statement " x is good " commonly functions in two ways at the same time. (1) It functions emotively as a favourable evaluation of x and an invitation to others to evaluate x favourably. (2) It functions descriptively as a statement that x has a certain attribute goodness. Most people do not distinguish these two functions. Consequently, if a person suggests that in its descriptive function the statement is false and should be withdrawn, they take him as also rejecting its emotive function, that is, refusing to favour and value x. And if a person generalizes this to suggest that there is no such attribute as independent goodness, they take this as a general refusal to approve or value anything.

An analogous situation arises with the words " right," " obligation," " duty," and so on. Here too the sentence " You ought to do x " has in ordinary life a double function. (1) It functions emotively as an evaluation of the choice whether to do x, and as bringing the speaker's influence on the hearer to make him do x, by way of the specifically moral emotions of approval and disapproval. (2) It functions descriptively, for it is thought to describe a fact. Here too the thinker who wishes to maintain that as a description this sentence corresponds to nothing actual is liable to find that his hearers take him as repudiating a moral demand; and the thinker who declares that there are no objective independent attributes of rightness and wrongness and obligatoriness finds himself being taken as repudiating all moral demands. Sir David Ross, for example, appears to have mistaken a denial of objectivism for a repudiation of all moral demands on page 28 of *The Foundations of Ethics*, especially when he wrote : " The denial of any distinction between right and wrong can usually be seen to be a disingenuous excuse for doing as one pleases."

I have known an objectivist to say to a subjectivist : " The plain truth seems to me to be that you are really denying that there are such things as obligations. But if you are I think you ought to say so." And the subjectivist may well tremble at such a remark ; for it is a quiet threat of what will happen to him if he does not acknowledge and obey society's moral demands upon him. The situation here is that, by means of the peculiar ambiguity in moral language, the objectivist is using the subjectivist's obedience to moral laws as a means of getting him to consent to a false description of the world. Let me make it crassly clear that I acknowledge and obey many moral demands, that I make many moral demands myself, that I am a very moralizing sort of person, that I often express my moral demands in the forms " you ought to do x " and " y is wrong " ; but that I hold that from these emotive uses of the words " ought " and " wrong " no true descriptive uses of them can be inferred, and nothing follows about what attributes occur in the world except that moral demands and emotions occur.

I have no desire to " discredit ethics," if by that phrase Sir David (*FE* 38) meant eradicating so far as possible all moral approval and disapproval. (I do, of course, like most people, desire to eradicate certain moral convictions. For example, I wish that all those who hold it would abandon the moral conviction that it is unmanly not to return injury for insult).

If a man says to me " Do you admit that promise-breaking is wrong ? " he is, in my opinion, whether he thinks so or not, doing at least this : he is demanding my disapproval of promise-breaking and my support of the rule against it. A very practical and serious matter, rather like asking me to sign an important document. But what kind of a document? A statement, such as an account of a collision I saw? Or a performance, to use Mr. Austin's word, such as a bequest? A performance; for disapproving promise-breaking and supporting the rule against it are performances, not statements. If the questioner is an ordinary man, I shall have no hesitation in answering " Yes, promise-breaking is wrong," that is, in expressing my moral feelings and my allegiance to the rule. But if my questioner is a philosophical objectivist, I am reluctant to answer yes because he will then take me as having made a statement, as having stated that a certain independent quality wrongness independently belongs to an act that has been done, whereas I think there is no evidence for such a quality. On the other hand, if I answer him no, meaning that there is no such objective quality as he has in mind, he takes me as an enemy of morality.

I say that there are such things as moral obligations. In saying that, I am uttering a general approval of the habits of making moral demands and acknowledging them and obeying them. Everybody else who utters this sentence is doing this too, whether he is conceptually aware that he is or not. I am not also trying to describe the world. I am doing the same sort of thing as when at my marriage I promised to cherish my wife, and not the same sort of thing as when I say there is meadow-sweet in England.

"But is there not a connexion between the emotive and the descriptive functions of sentences like " x is wrong " and " y is good " ? Is it not the case that persons, who come to believe that taken descriptively these sentences are always false, will come to feel that taken emotively they are always insincere? In other words, will not a man who comes to believe that there is no independent right or wrong or good or evil also come to feel indifference to other men's moral demands on him, and to feel no moral approval or disapproval in himself?"

The proposition here suggested is that " he who ceases to believe in independent right and good ceases to feel or make any moral demands ; he ceases to have any conscience." Before attempting to determine the truth value of this proposition, we ought, I suggest, to impress on ourselves the fact that its truth value makes no difference whatever to the truth value of the proposition that there is an independent right and an independent good.

(*a*) There is an independent right and an independent good.

(*b*) He who disbelieves proposition (*a*) gradually ceases to have a conscience.

It is important for us to keep in mind that these two propositions are independent ; that is to say, neither the truth nor the falsity of either would imply anything about the truth or falsity of the other. Suppose that we obtained evidence which made it reasonable to believe that proposition (*b*) was true ; that would not be the slightest justification for believing that proposition (*a*) was true, or for believing that it was false.

A person who disbelieved (*a*) and believed (*b*) might be in a very unpleasant position, namely if he both valued the spread of knowledge and valued people's having consciences. Because he valued the spread of knowledge, he would want to publish the fact that (*a*) was false, i.e., the fact that there was no independent right and no independent good. But he would also want to keep this fact secret, because he believed that its publication would lessen the prevalence of conscience, and he was against that.

But this unpleasant conflict would not be due to any logical connexion between the two propositions. There is no logical connexion between them ; they are independent. The conflict would be due to the facts that the man had more than one interest in life, and that, if a man has more than one interest in life, it is always possible for circumstances to arise in which he cannot satisfy one interest without dissatisfying another. The circumstance that, by a law of human nature, the disbelief in ethical objectivism tended to remove people's moral feelings, while ethical objectivism was false, would, if it were true, be a circumstance that would cause a conflict between the desire to spread knowledge and the desire to spread moral feeling.

I myself have both these desires, to spread knowledge and to spread moral feeling. If I were sure that I was confronted by an inevitable clash between them, I think I should gratify my desire to spread knowledge and thereby thwart my desire to spread moral feeling. I think the desire to spread knowledge, the love of truth as it is commonly called, takes precedence in me over the desire to spread the moral attitude. If I were uncertain whether a particular publication of truth would decrease the moral attitude, I should always give the benefit of the doubt to knowledge, and publish. This tendency is reinforced in me by the fact that one of the moral attitudes that I value and want to spread is the attitude that greatly approves sincerity and truth spreading and disapproves their opposites.

I see no good evidence that a belief in ethical subjectivism tends upon the whole either to weaken men's moral feelings, or to give them a new direction which I do not want, or to make men obey less often the moral feelings which they have. The effect of changing from an objectivist to a subjectivist view, upon one's moral feelings and one's obedience to them, seems to be upon the whole very slight. When and where such an effect occurs, it seems nearly always to consist in a slight strengthening of those moral feelings that are thought to accord with sympathy and benevolence, and a slight weakening of those moral feelings obedience to which seems to do nothing to alleviate the mass of human misery.

In the vast variety of human behaviour there are of course cases of the other sort. For example, persons whose morality has been indistinguishable from obeying orders, who think of duty merely as the command of some lawgiver external to themselves, and have the habit of obedience, may, if they come to disbelieve in the existence of this lawgiver, do selfish and low acts under the false impression that that is what their own nature demands. For a second example, clever adolescents becoming convinced of a subjectivist ethics occasionally adopt for a time what I think undesirable moral principles ; but this is a rare and fleeting occurrence. I suggest that such cases are rare, and by no means worthy to make us abandon our cherished liberal habit of freely spreading our honest opinions.

I have offered rebuttals of certain arguments against the emotive theory of ethics, namely the argument that believing the theory tends to make people immoral or nonmoral, the argument that you cannot approve of anything without thinking that it has the attribute goodness, and the argument that " if you think there is no such thing as obligation you ought to say so." I will now consider some more arguments against the emotive theory of ethics.

In *The Right and the Good* nearly all the emphasis falls on the question what we mean by these words, and very little on the question whether what we mean by them is actually found anywhere in the world. This state of affairs, combined with the obvious objectivism of the author, tends to suggest the following argument for objectivism and therefore against the emotive theory : " When we say that x is good, we mean that x has the independent attribute goodness ; what we mean must sometimes be true ; therefore the independent attribute goodness must sometimes occur." The question is whether you accept the second premiss, " what we mean must sometimes be true." It might be put in the form, " any attribute that we can refer to must be exemplified somewhere sometime."

In this form the argument would probably be championed by no one, since we can refer to the attribute of centaurhood without there being a centaur. But there is a modification which makes it more attractive : " When we say that x is good, we mean that x has the independent and unanalysable attribute goodness ; now we cannot refer to an unanalysable attribute unless it occurs sometime somewhere ; therefore the independent attribute goodness must sometimes occur." The principle here is that all simple concepts apply to something real. It is an old and oft believed principle, found for example both in Aristotle and Locke, and explicitly applied to the concept of goodness by Sir David Ross (*RG* 82) and to the concept of obligation by Dr. Ewing (*Mind* 1944 p. 135). I do not wish to try to persuade you now that it is a false principle. I will merely report my own belief that it is false and rests upon a false empiricism, namely the assumption that there is no way for an idea of a simple attribute to arise in a mind except through the direct and accurate impression of the wax of that mind by an example of the attribute occurring in reality. So much for that argument against ethical subjectivism which I inaccurately but briefly summarize to myself as the argument that " what we mean must be true."

The emotive theory of ethics completely escapes the argument that subjectivist theories are inconsistent with the obvious truth that men disagree and argue with each other about moral matters. Professor Stevenson shows clearly how it does so in his *Ethics and Language* (cc. i, v-viii). He distinguishes between disagreement in belief and disagreement in attitude. The sentence " I like democracy," and the reply " O I don't," are not logically inconsistent and need involve no disagreement in belief. But for all that they express a disagreement, namely a disagreement in attitude. And a disagreement in attitude may arouse far more feeling and assume much more importance than a disagreement in belief. We want our attitudes as well as our beliefs to be shared by others. An emotional conflict is more serious than a logical contradiction ; and the sentences " x is good " and " x is bad " together express an emotional conflict, whether or not they also express a logical contradiction. For the ethical attitudes are practical, active, militant. This is a more than sufficient explanation of our belief that we disagree on ethical matters.

Professor Stevenson goes on to show how there can be argument directed towards the resolution of disagreements in attitude as well as of disagreements in belief. He exemplifies and analyses 24 different types of ethical argument. Men's ethical attitudes are sometimes changed by changes in their beliefs ; and sometimes they are changed simply by the impact of other men's ethical attitudes. And both sorts of transaction may assume the argumentative form. The suggestion that subjectivist theories are inconsistent with the occurrence of ethical disagreements is persuasive only so long as we treat the function of ethical terms as solely descriptive (which Professor Moore and Sir David Ross and Dr. Ewing and also many subjectivists invariably do). It collapses entirely when we recognize that they have also an emotive function, and that there can be disagreement and argument in virtue of this function too.

The particular form of the emotive theory of ethics here advocated also escapes this objection in another way. For, since it allows that we intend an independent attribute when we use words like " good " or " right " (though we are mistaken in so doing), it makes it possible for two men to contradict each other logically when one asserts and the other denies that a certain act possesses the independent quality wrongness, which, they both assume, does belong to some act sometimes.

If we are habitually deceived in our use of ethical language, as is held by the form of the emotive theory here presented, the question arises why this is so, why we do not detect and reject the illusion ; and a failure to answer this might be thought to be evidence against the theory.

We can reply, first, that the same kind of pervasive error occurs, according to most of us, including most ethical objectivists, in our perception of the secondary qualities. We all habitually take certain colours and sounds as qualities belonging to objects in complete independence of the observer, and most of us on reflection hold that this is a mistake. This is not an explanation why the mistake in ethics occurs, but it is a consideration which makes it more probable that it does occur.

The cause of the mistake is probably multiple. Such a firmly persisting illusion would not arise from a single strand.

Some of the strands are probably analogous to some of the causes of the corresponding error in perception. For example, an experience which comes only in cognizing an object perhaps tends to be thought of as an attribute of that object; the aesthetic thrill, arising only when we are seeing or hearing or imagining or otherwise cognizing an object, tends to be thought of as a quality in that object. Beauty is pleasure objectified, as Santayana put it. Similarly, perhaps, the emotion of moral disapproval, arising only with the thought of some act, tends to suggest the presence of an independent quality wrongness in that act. If an experience comes only in cognizing an object, it can be controlled only through controlling the object. Only through the presentation and removal of objects, either in fact or in imagination, can I control my aesthetic feelings, or my feelings of esteem and abhorrence. What comes to me only through objects is liable to seem to belong to the objects.

Another cause, which works to produce the mistake in ethics but not in perception, is the greater authority of the objective language. Our evaluative emotions, and still more our moral emotions, are practical. They aim at altering feeling and behaviour. They therefore seek authority, all the authority they can get. But the sentence " I disapprove of x " is much less authoritative than the sentence " x is wrong," if the latter is taken as a description of an independent fact which is somehow compulsive upon action. As Professor Mackie puts it, " we want everyone to adopt our approvals, and this will most surely come about if they have only to perceive a genuinely existing objective fact, for what we feel is in general private, what we perceive may be common to all. Suppose that we approve of hard work: then if as well as a feeling of approval in our minds there were an objective fact like ' hard work is good,' such that everyone could observe the fact and such that the mere observation would arouse in him a like feeling of approval, and even perhaps stimulate him to work, we should eventually get what we want done; people would work hard." (*Austral J. of Psych. & Philos.* XXIV 82. In adopting this suggestion from Professor Mackie I want to remark that I do not adopt all the value-attitudes expressed or implied in his article, and especially not the title " A Refutation of Morals," which unfortunately suggests a repudiation of all moral demands.)

The great reason in favour of the emotive theory of ethics is economy. The ocurrence of emotive language, and of human feelings of approval and disapproval, is a fact in any case. If this fact by itself will explain human behaviour and speech in the matter of morals and valuation, it is unreasonable to hypothesize any further fact, consisting in the appearance from time to time of the " non-natural " qualities wrongness and badness and the rest.

A lesser reason in favour of the emotive theory of ethics is that it relieves us of the necessity of believing in intuition in ethics, which is repugnant to many of us. That intuition is essential to the objectivist view is fully admitted by Sir David Ross and Dr. Ewing, who are I suppose the chief living defenders of objectivism since Professor Moore began to express doubts. Any knowledge of objective ethical facts must rest on a direct non-perceptual non-logical knowledge of an a priori synthetic ethical proposition. We have little difficulty in believing in perceptual intuition, in that by my sense-experience I apprehend a fact without inferring it. We have little difficulty in believing in logical intuition, in that from the definitions of the terms in a proposition I see that the proposition must be true because its contradictory contradicts itself. But we have great difficulty in believing in an intuition which is neither of these, which is guaranteed neither by the mere definitions of the terms nor by a sense-experience.

There is no check on such an intuition. There is no method by which men's accounts of their intuitions of this sort may be progressively brought into agreement. If I suspect that a man has misdescribed what he saw, I can sometimes go with him to the place, reinstate the seeing, and reach agreement with him about the correct description of that seeing. But if I suspect that he has misdescribed the ethical intuition which he says he has had, there is nothing to be done. Argument on fundamental moral and axiological doctrines is impossible if the objectivist view be true. Yet the most intimate experience, the most compelling experience, the most vivid experience, can be misdescribed by its enjoyer. It often is misdescribed, and in good faith, and with intense conviction that the description is correct. I cannot share Bishop Gore's opinion that intuition is as respectable a method of getting knowledge about reality as scientific induction ; and I am the reverse of persuaded by his view that one of the criteria for distinguishing good intuitions from bad is that the good ones give you strength. (*Belief in God*).

In *Principia Ethica* Professor Moore introduced a method which looks like a procedure for reaching agreement on ethical intuitions. He called it the " method of isolation " (*PE* 93, 94, 187, 197). It consists in determining whether x is intrinsically good by imagining a universe consisting of x alone, and bringing one's ethical intuition to bear on that ; or in determining whether x is intrinsically better than y, by comparing an imaginary universe consisting solely of x with another consisting solely of y. This method was extensively used both by its inventor and by Sir David Ross (e.g. *RG* 138). All our evaluations of extrinsic goods and evils are based, it was held, on our evaluations of intrinsic goods and evils ; and all the latter are to be determined, if we follow *Principia Ethica*, by the method of isolation.

I rebel against this method of deciding what is good and what is bad ; and I think a great many other people must do so too. If I ever think I have any ethical intuition, at least I know it evaporates when I place myself in these artificial imaginary situations. Asking me to isolate x and then intuit whether it is good seems like asking a man to keep still while you remove the support on which he rests.

The results achieved by this method in *Principia Ethica* and *The Right and the Good* throw further suspicion on the method. These brief lists of four or five sorts, are they all that the world offers of good kinds of thing ? Must I be referring only to extrinsic goodness when I call a hammer good, or a cheese, or a satire? Are my emotions essentially inappropriate if I enjoy a good hammer as such, and do not immediately pass on to the thought of some intrinsic good to which a hammer might lead?

From my subjective point of view, the essential unsatisfactoriness of these objectivist answers to the question what things are good lies in their disregarding our habit of esteeming or cherishing x because x leads to y. The objectivist's distinction of goods into intrinsic suggests a corresponding twofold distinction of our emotions: when x is an intrinsic good, we esteem it; when x is an extrinsic good, we do not esteem it, but merely recognize intellectually that it is a means to an intrinsic good, and esteem the intrinsic good. Our actual emotions, however, frequently realize a third possibility, to which nothing in the objectivist scheme corresponds: we esteem and cherish x as such, though we should not do so if we did not think that x led to some other good. If a man esteems and cherishes x as such, he naturally expresses this by saying " x is good," and he does not want to admit that he merely means that x leads to something good. Yet, if you convince him that x leads to no good, or is useless, he no longer esteems it. The method of isolation therefore does not tell us what we actually value and esteem. And when we ask ourselves what things are good, surely we want to know what we actually esteem as such, not what we should esteem in some other universe.

It is a feature of the lists of goods in *Principia Ethica* and *The Right and the Good* that human consciousness enters into them all. This contrasts with the fact that we commonly call good many things of which human consciousness is no part, such as a hammer or a plant. In my opinion, this departure from ordinary language is brought upon the objectivists by their theory. Having refused to accept any reference to the evaluating subject in their account of how we use the word " good," they are led to include the subject in every good thing, and thus to narrow the list of good things paradoxically. If, however, we hold that ethical language is primarily the expression and propagation of the speaker's own evaluations, we are free to say that the speaker may judge favourably not merely states of consciousness but anything whatever, so that, when he sincerely says that " x is intrinsically good," x may be of any sort ; and this accords much better with our ordinary idea that the world is full of many kinds of bad thing and many kinds of good thing.

II. *By* H. J. Paton.

The emotive theory of ethics, if I may try to sum up Mr. Robinson's version of it, maintains something like this. When men make judgments of value and particularly of ethical value, when, for example, they assert that X is good, they believe that they are ascribing to X an unanalysable quality which belongs to it in complete independence of all human feelings and thoughts. In this they are mistaken, for there is no such unanalysable quality. Hence they are, even if unconsciously, using the word " good " emotively, not descriptively : that is to say, they are using it to express and to evoke an emotion, not to describe anything ; and since nothing is being described, the emotion in question is independent of anything described, and is roused only by the word " good " itself.

Mr. Robinson's exposition and defence of this doctrine may be taken as an attempt to set forth briefly the position worked out in greater detail by Professor Stevenson in his *Ethics and Language*. Our concern is therefore with the theory as a whole, and we may legitimately interpret Mr. Robinson's paper in the light of the larger work. What we are being asked to do is to adopt a special form of ethical subjectivism in place of ethical objectivism. This invitation, in spite of the persuasiveness of its authors, I am unable to accept.

If we look first at ethical objectivism, we may note two points of special interest in Mr. Robinson's treatment—points which I take to be peculiarly his own.

In the first place Mr. Robinson seems to assume that if we are objectivists in ethics, we must hold goodness to be an unanalysable attribute or quality belonging to things in complete independence of all human feelings and thoughts. He does, it is true, say in one place that in the objectivist view goodness may be either definable or indefinable ; but for purposes of his argument he takes it for granted that if he can disprove the contention that goodness is an unanalysable quality, he has *ipso facto* disposed of objectivism.

The view that goodness is an unanalysable and indefinable quality dates from the year 1903. Nothing has been more remarkable in my philosophical experience than the way in which this doctrine first acquired popularity and then lost it. Even its author appears almost to have abandoned it. It is a doctrine which I have never been able to support, but I could wish that some one were present to defend it to-day. It was at least an attempt to do justice to the objectivity claimed by ethical judgments and to the real difficulties encountered in any attempt to define goodness. I have no wish to question the criticisms proffered by Mr. Robinson, but his assumption that we have to choose between this kind of objectivism and his own brand of subjectivism is one which cannot be accepted. We may note with interest how easy it is to pass from extreme objectivism to extreme subjectivism; but we must remember that the objectivist doctrine was defended for more than two thousand years before it was connected with a simple indefinable unanalysable quality or attribute. To refute one of its latest accretions is by no means to refute it.

The second point of special interest in Mr. Robinson's treatment of objectivism is one which will, I hope, find something like general approval. If it does, we shall at least have some agreement as to the *prima facie* description of the subject under discussion. Mr. Robinson holds that in common speech we do in fact use ethical words like " right " and " good " descriptively: that is, on his view, we use them in order to name an independent, unanalysable attribute. He adds, however, that to say this is to make actual usage rather more precise than it in fact is.

This interpretation of ordinary usage is, I suggest, too precise in attributing to the ordinary man a belief in unanalysable qualities. I should prefer to say that the ordinary man in judging " This is good " assumes that it is good whatever he happens to feel or even to think about it. He believes that his judgment is true, and that other people, if their judgments are true, will judge as he does. If I may put this in my own language, the ordinary ethical judgment makes a claim to objectivity (a claim to be valid for all men so far as they are rational). More precisely, the ordinary man takes it for granted that it is possible to judge in accordance with objective ethical principles and to act in accordance with these principles. Even if he does not know it reflectively, he is an objectivist in ethics.

This admission—and I take it Mr. Robinson makes an admission roughly of this kind—is important if we attach any value to common sense at least as a starting point for enquiry. It follows that on his theory there is, as he says, " a pervasive tendency to error in our ordinary ethical language " : we are " habitually deceived in our use of ethical language." We may reasonably display caution in accepting a theory which admittedly runs counter to the initial empirical evidence ; and we may reasonably ask—since the theory professes to be based on an analysis of language—whether we are being offered an analysis of language as it is actually used, or as it would be used if it were used differently.

Thus far my contention is merely that if objectivism is to be refuted, it must be refuted *generally* : it is not enough to refute a particular specialised precise form of it. On the other hand, if subjectivism is to be defended, it must be defended in a more precise form than that given to it either by Mr. Robinson or by Professor Stevenson. At its present stage the doctrine suffers from vagueness : it fails to make necessary distinctions, and it lumps together things that are very different. My illustrations of this must be brief and consequently dogmatic.

(1) We want to be told more precisely what it is that ethical language in its emotive use is supposed at once to express and to evoke. Is it a feeling ? Is it an emotion ? Is it an attitude ? These terms seem to be used indifferently. The positivistic doctrine, as expounded by Professor Ayer, speaks only of feelings and emotions, and it seemed to me a real improvement when Professor Stevenson began to speak of attitudes. Unfortunately it is impossible to discover what is meant by this terminology, and Professor Stevenson appears deliberately to blur the distinction be-

tween feeling and willing by speaking of " affective-conative" attitudes. No one need deny that ethical judgments are accompanied in some degree by emotion, but so are non-ethical judgments. The essential characteristic of ethical judgments is that they are connected in some way with a conative attitude or—as I prefer to say—with an attitude of will.

(2) We are no better off when stress is laid, as it often is, on an attitude of *approval*. " Approval " is one of the vaguest words in the English language. " I approve " may mean " I have a certain sort of feeling " (or a disposition to certain sorts of feeling). It may mean " I favour " (or have a disposition to favour) ; and this may be taken to assert or to manifest an attitude of will. But " I approve of X " may also mean " I think or believe that X is good "— that is, it may be understood as cognitive and as claiming to assert what is true. This last I take to be its primary meaning. Etymologically " approval " is connected with proving or putting to the proof. It is the very ambiguity of the word which gives plausibility to Professor Stevenson's analysis.

(3) If we are offering an analysis of linguistic usage, we must examine the different senses in which the word " good " is used, and we must try to trace some connexion between these different senses. If we lump all the senses together, we are likely to get a false understanding of the word by taking it on its least distinctive level. " This is good " may mean " This is pleasant," as when we say " This is a good cheese." It may mean " This is beautiful (or aesthetically successful)," as when we say " This is a good satire." But in its *specific* meaning the word " good " is opposed to the words " pleasant " and " beautiful "— it is because of this opposition that we employ three different words. On this level " good " may mean " good for " (a good hammer) or " good at " (a good cricketer) ; it may mean " my good " or " good for me "—good as contributing to my happiness or welfare ; and it may mean " morally good " (a good man). It is in these *distinctive* senses that " good " becomes connected, not with feeling, but with an

attitude of will and with the *concept* of some sort of teleological system. It is in these senses that our particular judgments of goodness claim objectivity as falling under a concept or rule of some kind, whereas our judgments of pleasantness or even of beauty make no appeal to any concept, and such claims to objectivity as they have are not claims to be valid for rational agents as such. Unless we follow up these (and possibly other) distinctions, we can have no satisfactory theory of goodness, and still less of moral goodness. When Professor Stevenson tells us that the moral senses of ethical terms " raise no special problems of ethics or methodology," he indicates clearly enough that whatever else we may learn from him (and we may learn much), we need expect little help in understanding the difference between moral and non-moral action.

(4) The emotive theory is based on the assumption that linguistic usage must be either descriptive or emotive. Here again the word " emotive " is so blurred that it seems to mean little more than " non-descriptive." If we suppose that we know what is meant by " descriptive " (and I am not sure that I do), there are many kinds of non-descriptive linguistic usages. Of these the one that would most naturally be described as " emotive " is the aesthetic use (as in poetry) ; but our ethical judgments are not lyrical, and our poetic creations are not practical. Again, our ethical judgments are sometimes assimilated on this theory to imperatives or quasi-imperatives. But these are not (like poetic utterances) intended to express or to evoke emotion : they are intended primarily to elicit action. In spite of the emphasis laid on imperatives, Professor Stevenson refuses to connect emotive meaning with action : connexion with action is regarded—very paradoxically—as the distinguishing mark of *descriptive* meaning. Mr. Robinson is nearer the truth when he speaks of an ethical judgment as a " performance." But if it is a performance, why should he describe it as emotive ? The modern French existentialists would regard it as a personal choice, and their theory, whatever be its defects, is more precise and closer to the facts.

For all these reasons the emotive theory requires a good deal of clarification before it can be readily accepted. I hope that if it were clarified it would begin to look rather different. Its present value lies mainly in its protest against the intellectualism of modern ethical theory. Ethical judgments are not merely intellectual or theoretical, and it is very necessary to point this out. But the natural reaction from extreme intellectualism is emotionalism, and the natural reaction from extreme ethical realism is ethical subjectivism (or ethical scepticism). The emotive theory illustrates these reactions and tends to fall into even worse extremes. Judgments of goodness are not based on blind personal emotions. We have only to look at judgments of utility or skill to see this at once, and this is one reason why it is advisable to study judgments of this kind. The emotive theory is at its best when it begins to talk, not about emotion, but about attitudes (however vaguely understood) and about performance. If ethical judgments are bound up with an attitude of will, we can understand how they are accompanied by emotions inseparable from the pursuit of any end and from success or failure in its attainment. We can understand also how they may give rise to a harmony or conflict of wills and to the powerful emotions attendant upon such a harmony or conflict. It is highly necessary to distinguish between agreement (or disagreement) in belief and agreement (or disagreement) in attitude. Emphasis on this distinction is the chief merit of Professor Stevenson's book, though I fail to understand why he consistently assumes agreement in attitude to be good. He even assumes that " enlightened " agreement is better than agreement which is not enlightened. In so doing he seems either to be assuming unconsciously some objective standard of goodness or else to be introducing personal preferences into a " neutral " analysis in which they should have no place.

The central defect of the emotive theory is its failure to distinguish clearly between attitudes of will and mere emotions. Emotions are essentially non-rational. We have to understand them in the light of their causes, and when we speak of the " reasons " for them we mean only the causes of which they are the psychological effects: we do not regard them as following from rational principles consciously understood and deliberately adopted. All of this, which is true enough of emotions, and indeed of impulses and desires, is transferred by Professor Stevenson—if I understand him aright—to attitudes, and so to ethical judgments, and so to volition and action. I do not know how Mr. Robinson views this doctrine, but although it is widely taken for granted at the present time, I believe that it is remote from the truth.

It may be objected to this interpretation that Professor Stevenson is prepared to speak of "*reasons*" which "support" our ethical judgments and that he distinguishes these reasons from other means of influencing such judgments—means grouped together under the head of "persuasion." But strangely enough, they are called "reasons" only because they are purely *theoretical* beliefs about matters of fact and consequently beliefs which can be influenced by reasoning. Their relation to our ethical judgments is neither that between ground and consequent nor that between observations and the generalisations based on them; and since it is neither of these logical relations, it is assumed to be a purely psychological one—a relation of psychological cause and effect. Ethical judgments are in themselves altogether non-rational on this theory.

It would take too long to argue out this question here—I have tried to do so elsewhere. The doctrine would be relatively harmless if it were merely an arbitrary attempt to limit the usage of the word "rational," but it goes much deeper than this. It assumes a divorce between thinking and acting which verges on the fantastic, and it is astonishing as coming from any one who has been influenced by pragmatism. Such a divorce corresponds to nothing in my experience, and it seems to me obvious that intelligence (or stupidity) is manifested in actions and in practical judgments just as much as it is in theoretical judgments. It would be astonishing if we were rational in thinking out the cause of a desired effect, but wholly non-rational in judging that it offered us the best means to a chosen end and in choosing it as such a means. Professor Stevenson himself recognises that an ethical judgment made by one man about X will " instinctively " be taken to cover the *class* of objects in which X falls. This presence of the concept or rule in our judgments of goodness seems to me one of the essential marks of their rationality. To ascribe it to " instinct " is to beg a very important question.[1]

So brief a statement cannot do justice to the subtleties of Professor Stevenson's arguments, and equally it cannot do justice to my own position. Nevertheless this question seems to me the fundamental question for moral philosophy. Those who believe in practical reason are not defending some " mysterious " faculty concerned with an " occult " subject matter. Emotive terms of this sort as used by Professor Stevenson—and they are a rare indulgence on his part—merely obscure the issue. The objectivist claim which he has to refute is this—that the same intelligence which he himself recognises to be manifested in theoretical enquiries is also manifested, with appropriate differences, in volitions and in the judgments of value which are inseparable from volition.

Professor Stevenson recognises two patterns of ethical analysis. As a " working model " of the first we may take the following : " This is good " means " *I approve of this; do so as well.*"

Mr. Robinson warns us that we have in this no exact equivalence : there are few or no emotive synonyms (though there are emotive tautologies). Nevertheless, if we add certain qualifications which must here be omitted, we may, I presume, take this as a sort of abstract schema for the neutral and detached analysis of ethical judgments.

The first part " I approve of this " is supposed to represent the *descriptive* element in the judgment. " This is good." Apart from the ambiguity, already noted, of the word " approve " I do not think that " This is good " *means* " I approve of this "—any more than " This is square " *means* " I think this is square." At the most it may be said

---

[1] See *Ethics and Language*, p. 95.

that some statement about my state of mind is suggested or implied in both cases, but it is unnatural to regard this as the primary descriptive meaning. Furthermore—and I think this is Mr. Russell's view—" I approve of this " might be regarded better as "*expressing*" than as "*describing*" the speaker's state of mind in the judgment " This is good." If so, it is concerned with the subjective factor, and Professor Stevenson has got this side of his schematic equivalence precisely wrong in connecting it with the objective factor.

The second part " Do so as well " is regarded as belonging to the *emotive* side of the judgment " This is good." I do not think this imperative represents only, or even mainly, the emotive aspect of the judgment. The ethical judgment, like other judgments, claims to be valid, not merely for the person who makes it, but for other persons as well. This is what we mean by saying that it claims to be objective, and this claim is not unnaturally expressed in an imperative addressed to other people. As Mr. Russell has said,[2] " in adult life all speech . . is in the imperative mood. When it seems to be a mere statement, it should be prefaced by the words ' Know that.' " Here again Professor Stevenson seems to have reversed the subjective and objective sides of the judgment he is analysing. In ethical judgments the imperative form has an additional plausibility if the claim to objectivity is a claim to be valid, not merely for the thoughts, but for the wills, of others. This does not in any way weaken the claim to objectivity. It does, however, mean that there must also be some special sort of subjective emotional accompaniment; and it is perhaps because Professor Stevenson fails to distinguish between the imperative and the emotive use of language that he supposes this element in his analysis to be purely subjective.

The working model for the second schematic pattern of ethical analysis is as follows : " ' This is good ' has the meaning of ' This has qualities or relations X, Y, Z . . . ' ' except that ' good ' has as well a laudatory emotive mean-

---

[2] *An enquiry into Meaning and Truth*, pp. 26–7.

ing which permits it to express the speaker's approval, and tends to evoke the approval of the hearer."

The details of this need not here concern us, though it may be noted that the speaker's approval is now "*expressed*" (and not "*described*," as it was in the first pattern). The essential point is this. All that Professor Stevenson says about the second pattern follows from what he has said about the first. Once we assert that judgments of goodness are emotive, then to define " good " by reference to any describable qualities can only be to direct emotion to these qualities. Consequently the definition must be merely " persuasive " in his sense : it is not neutral, and it is not clarificatory. To choose a definition of this kind is merely " to plead a cause."

What is the result ? Professor Stevenson—and in this he is entirely consistent—is telling us that to define " good " by connecting it with anything objective, and particularly with any objective standards, *must be ruled out from the start* : if we attempt to do this, we are confusing analysis with emotive valuation. This is not a *further* argument against objectivity—it is merely a further consequence of rejecting objectivity on what seem to me to be *a priori* grounds. The most it can show is that you can still give some sort of plausible analysis of ethical judgments and definitions when you have denied objective standards. If we regard this denial as a mistake, the second pattern will be seen merely to develop further the errors already present in the first.

What are the reasons why we should accept this emotive theory of ethics ? It has a certain attraction for men who in a period of war and revolution have lost their bearings and become disillusioned about the practicability, and even about the value, of previously accepted ideals. In this respect it bears a certain resemblance to its wilder brother, the existentialist doctrine of Sartre and others in France. It may seem to be the only alternative if we suppose objectivism in ethics to mean that precisely the same moral rules hold absolutely, without any relation to changing circumstances. Such a belief, however, rests upon the assumption that objectivism is incompatible with any form of relativity.

This assumption is mistaken since ultimate moral principles must, on any sensible view, be applied differently in different circumstances. In Mr. Robinson's case the main ground for accepting the emotive theory is apparently dissatisfaction with the doctrines of Professor G. E. Moore, and this contention has already been considered. He also, like Professor Stevenson, seems to take it for granted that no statement can be true unless it is based on the observational methods of empirical science. If no statement can be true unless it can in principle be verified by intuition (perhaps even by sensuous intuition) and can be said to describe a " fact " regarded as something " actual," then clearly a statement such as " You ought to do X " cannot be true ; for it does not even profess to describe what actually is but what ought to be.

It would be foolish to deny that there are great and special difficulties about the status of judgments of value or obligation, and this no doubt is the strength of the emotive theory. But these difficulties will not be solved merely by defining words like " true " or " objective " in such a way that the truth of these judgments is ruled out from the start. Mr. Robinson admits—and it is a mark of candour—that in ordinary usage these judgments do claim to be true. We have to look at this problem for its own sake and on its own merits and not to dismiss it on the *a priori* ground that—by definition—only the factual judgments of empirical science can be true. From the point of view of language it is no good telling us that in the usage of empirical science there are no evaluative words and that consequently any use of such words must be merely emotive. To exclude colour words from our language is not to abolish colours. I do not say this is an exact parallel, but I do say that the present study of language is too narrowly confined and is so far likely to be misleading. It is initially less likely that " we are habitually deceived in our use of ethical language " than that the emotive theorists are mistaken.

Arguments based on what seem to be arbitrary definitions leave a feeling of frustration in those who cannot accept the conclusions, and this perhaps can be illustrated by applying similar methods to the word " true " itself. The argument might run something like this. It has commonly been assumed that in the statement " This proposition is true " we are ascribing to the proposition an unanalysable quality and so are describing an actual fact. In this, however, we are deceived, for no such unanalysable quality is given to sensuous intuition or indeed to any kind of intuition. We must reject such " non-natural qualities " and abandon the appeal to " other-worldly mystery." Those who have held such theories have failed to notice the strongly emotive character of the word " true " ; and since this word cannot be used descriptively, it must be used emotively. We must therefore consider what is common to all usages of the word, and although people sometimes speak of mathematical truth, of scientific truth, of historical truth, even of artistic and moral and religious truth, these different usages raise no special problems. A detached analysis can take as its first working model a schema of this form : " This proposition is true " means " I approve of this proposition ; do so as well ". It can also recognise, but not use, definitions of the form " This proposition is true " means " This proposition has the characteristic of being verifiable by sense-perception or of being coherent with other propositions or of being what works, and so on !; to which it must be added that the word " true " has a laudatory meaning enabling it to express the speaker's approval and to evoke a similar approval in the hearer. All such definitions are persuasive and have no place in any neutral analysis, though as normative epistemologists we are fully entitled to adopt any of them. We may feel dissatisfied at first with this theory, but the dissatisfaction will disappear once our psychological mechanism has been adjusted, and everything will go on exactly as it did before.

I am not suggesting that this is a precise parallel, and it must by its very brevity do less than justice to the skill and care with which the emotive theory has been worked out. But the emotions it is not unlikely to arouse may perhaps convey to those who reject it something of the dissatisfaction felt with regard to the emotive theory by those who believe that unless morality admits of objective standards, then there is no such thing as morality at all.

Here we come to the practical question, one of considerable delicacy. Both Professor Stevenson and Mr. Robinson are sensitive to the charge that they are working to " discredit ethics." No reasonable man acquainted with their arguments will maintain that they are doing anything to discredit ethics. The serious question we have to ask ourselves—and I say this not unkindly—is whether their doctrine does not discredit morality.

We are assured by both these gentlemen that an affirmative answer can be based only on misunderstanding, and Mr. Robinson hints that it is likely to be given only by a nasty sort of person, willing to back up his answer with " quiet threats." I trust I shall not be suspected of this if I say that in my opinion these doctrines do discredit morality. The misunderstanding on this matter seems to be found on the other side.

It would be absurd to say of the emotive theory that it discredits morality, *as morality is understood by the emotive theory*. But that is not the charge which is brought. The charge is, on the contrary, that it discredits morality as it is understood by the objectivist (and, if we can agree with Mr. Robinson, as it is understood by the ordinary man). It is obvious on the face of it that discrediting morality in this sense is what the emotive theory " does absolutely nothing else but."

This is not a mere matter of words, but of serious practical importance. Suppose I believe, as I do believe, that a morally good action is one done for the sake of duty, done in order to obey a law which is independent of my likings and dislikings ; and suppose I believe that to obey this law for its own sake is to realise a value in comparison with which the satisfaction of my personal desires is insignificant ; it is then obvious that to accept Mr. Robinson's doctrines would make morally good action impossible. The emotive theory undermines the very foundations of morality (not to mention religion). Mr. Robinson ought not to be surprised if some people display a shade of vehemence in their criticisms. It seems to them that if his doctrines are true, then life is merely trivial.

No doubt he does not discredit morality as he understands morality. But how does he understand morality? I confess I do not know. He speaks of "moral feelings," "moral demands," "moral approval and disapproval," and so on. But how does he distinguish these from feelings, demands, and so on, which are not moral? The word "ethical" he extends in such a way that "good" in all its various senses may be called an "ethical" adjective. I doubt whether his employment of the word "moral" is so catholic (or so indiscriminate), yet I do not think that he has explained (or Professor Stevenson either) how a more restricted usage fits in with the emotive theory. Indeed, as I understand his view, moral approval, like any other form of approval, has a cause, but no ground or principle, and consequently is merely contingent; and since it is an affective-conative attitude, not a judgment claiming truth, we should describe it less misleadingly if we called it "liking" or "wishing" or "wanting" instead of "approval". I do not wish to use emotive terms, but only to make my interpretation clear, when I say that in this theory "I approve" means "I happen to like"—"I" of course referring to an indefinite I. In my own language "I approve morally" is fundamentally *opposed* to "I happen to like," and "I happen to like morally" is a contradiction in terms. When I say that an action is morally good, I am at least attempting to rise above my contingent personal likes and dislikes, and I believe this to conform with ordinary usage. I can understand the emotive theory when it is applied to the judgment "This is a good cheese." I can understand it (though I cannot accept it) if it holds that the judgment "This is a morally good action" is the same in kind. If, on the other hand, the doctrine is that the moral judgment differs in kind, we ought to be told what the difference is. In one place Mr. Robinson speaks as if in order to make a moral judgment I have only to examine my desires and to decide which of them "takes precedence in me." What is meant by "takes precedence" in such a context?

If we pass over this obscurity, we may perhaps suppose that we are roughly agreed on the kinds of action to which the word " moral " is in fact applied, even although we do not understand the connotation it has for Mr. Robinson, and might differ from him profoundly if we could understand it. On this supposition we may take Mr. Robinson to say something like this. If we change from an objectivist view to a subjectivist one, we shall in all probability continue to approve (that is, to like) the actions hitherto called " moral "; we shall continue to approve them as strongly as before ; and we shall continue to act on these approvals just as much as before. The last point may be expressed by saying that we shall continue to act " conscientiously."

Even if all this were true—and I hope it is—the so-called " moral " actions would have no value other than that of satisfying my contingent desires, and so—unless I am misunderstanding the position—they would not be moral actions at all. Apart from the question of value, the question of fact can be settled only empirically : all that Mr. Robinson or I can say about it is based on our judgment of probabilities. Yet even here we must draw a further distinction. If men were following contingent desires merely as they happened to occur at any moment, they would obviously behave quite otherwise than they commonly do at present. At the back of his mind Professor Stevenson seems to assume that men aim at some sort of harmonious or systematic satisfaction of their contingent desires, and I hope Mr. Robinson does the same. To make Mr. Robinson's contention at all plausible we must assume men to be moved at least by an enlightened self-interest which is not necessarily selfish but seeks to satisfy systematically our social, as well as our non-social, desires. This idea of system seems to me a mark of rationality in man, which is already fatal to the emotive theory, but into this we need not enter. On this assumption I have no wish to deny that self-interest—especially if I have been well brought up and meet with no great temptation—may lead me to act very much as I did when I believed in (and too often failed to follow) objective standards not determined by my likings and dislikings.

I have no wish even to deny that in propitious circumstances the clash of opposing self-interests may establish, at a great cost in suffering, some kind of uneasy equilibrium not wholly unlike that which would be attained if most men were acting conscientiously on the principle of considering others as well as themselves. Nevertheless one of the influences leading to our present standards of conduct has been, as Mr. Robinson admits, the belief that these standards are objective ; and I am pretty sure that if we all abandoned this belief, we should tend (though perhaps not immediately) to feel and act differently. He recognises himself that what he calls " the objective language " has " greater authority." It has this greater authority, not through any mere magic, but precisely because it is objective ; and although the emotive theorists propose themselves to use the objective language in practice, its authority both for themselves and for others will be greatly diminished once we realise that it is being used in so Pickwickian a sense. This can hardly happen without a weakening of " moral " feelings and a tendency to obey such feelings less often (if we can be said to obey feelings) when they are opposed to feelings commonly regarded as " immoral." My experience suggests that though men act wrongly even when they accept objective standards, they act more wrongly when a belief in objective standards is removed. I do not want to be unfair to Mr. Robinson, but I believe that his theory plays into the hands of the demonic types who have brought the world to its present pass, and whose contingent approvals and disapprovals have more emotive force than the contingent approvals and disapprovals of peaceful men like Mr. Robinson and myself. I can see little hope for the spread of " moral " action in the world unless we are prepared to accept and to act upon a law which we believe holds for all men alike and bids us treat others, not simply as a means to the satisfaction of our own contingent desires, but as ends in their own right. To accept and to act upon such a law as binding upon all men is to adopt in action a principle which is objective, not merely in the sense that it treats myself and others impartially, but in the sense that it springs from a reason which necessarily manifests its impartiality in acting (as in thinking) and is distinct from any merely contingent desire.

The practical effect of abandoning such a principle of objectivity can be settled decisively only by observation and experiment. But an experiment with general subjectivism is a ticklish matter. We may perhaps see such an experiment—I rather think we have been seeing it in recent years. We shall be fortunate if it does not end in the crash of our civilisation.

Mr. Robinson assures us that even if my judgment of probabilities were correct, it would offer no ground whatever for asserting the truth of the objectivist doctrine.

On his own definition of " truth," this contention may well be correct. He is, I assume, still taking it for granted that the objectivist doctrine can be " true " only if it can be verified by some sort of intuition of an unanalysable and independent quality or attribute to which we give the name of " goodness." As I see it, the problem before us is very different. What we are concerned to know is whether certain ultimate principles of action are valid for, or binding upon, all men so far as they are rational. There are admittedly great difficulties in establishing such a proposition, but these have nothing to do with the independent existence of unanalysable qualities. If such a proposition could be established, I should be inclined to call it " true," even if this does not conform to Mr. Robinson's definition of " truth." In fact I must call it " true " till I am supplied with a better word, though I am willing to keep an open mind on the status of such a proposition and on the best way to describe that status.

If we thus extend the meaning of the word " true," are we certain that the " truth " of such propositions is wholly unrelated to facts about the activities supposed to be governed by the principles in question?

Suppose I lay down the proposition that the thinking of rational agents must be self consistent if it is to be true. I am acquainted with what I call " true " thinking in the empirical sciences and in history. Is it wholly irrelevant to my contention if I can show that empirical science and history do follow the principle of self-consistency and that they would collapse if they abandoned it? If I could show this, should I not be doing more than merely stating arbitrarily that I refused to give the name of "science" or "history" to anything inconsistent with my principle? Should I not be establishing some sort of *prima facie* case for the "truth" of my original proposition?

Suppose I lay down the proposition that the actions of rational agents must be willed in accordance with the principle of objectivity if they are to be morally good. I am acquainted with what I call "morally good" actions. Is it wholly irrelevant if I can show, not merely that they do follow this principle (as Mr. Robinson is good enough to admit), but that they would collapse if they abandoned it? If I could do this, should I not be establishing some sort of *prima facie* case for the "truth" of my original proposition?

Whatever be the correct theory in this difficult matter, the relation between facts and principles does not seem so simple to me as it does to Mr. Robinson. If we turn to practice, we have good grounds for adopting, and for recommending, principles which are necessary to successful achievement either in thought or in action, even although we may be unable to justify them otherwise. My main contention, however, is that the principles of acting are on the same sort of footing as the principles of thinking and that they have an equal claim to be examined independently. It is a mistake first to determine and adopt the presuppositions of empirical science and then to infer as a corollary what the presuppositions of good action must be. Yet I think that it is precisely this method which has led to positivistic doctrines about morality.

These difficult logical problems I have no wish to pursue further. I wish to insist only on one thing. If we are convinced that objective principles are essential to good action as well as to right thinking, we must refuse to abandon this belief merely because it is ruled out by certain definitions of words like "true" and "good." We are all the less inclined to abandon it when we are assured that definitions are arbitrary or verbal. Mr. Robinson recognises definition to be something more than verbal; and he tells us that what purports to be the definition of an attribute is sometimes a proposal that we should think about a slightly different attribute in future. With all respect, this is what he seems to me to be doing in his paper—with the difference that the attribute he asks us to think about in future is not slightly, but totally, different from moral goodness, as we understand it, and indeed from *any* kind of goodness in any *distinctive* sense of that word.

I should, however, like in conclusion to come as near to Mr. Robinson's position as I can. We are agreed in holding theoretically (probably with some differences) that a judgment of goodness is not purely intellectual but involves in some way an attitude of will. We should probably agree in practice that if a man is to be morally good he must consider others as well as himself. So far, this is a subjective principle or maxim which we have in common even if we too often fail to follow it in action. We should both like other people to follow it. But for Mr. Robinson this maxim is the product of merely contingent circumstances (including no doubt a knowledge of facts as well as pressure of various kinds from society, temperament, and so on). It has no claim to rank above very different maxims which are due to other contingent circumstances and are adopted by other men—for example, the maxim that any action is good if it furthers the interests of the master race or the class struggle. I cannot accept this doctrine any more than I can accept a doctrine which puts on the same level the judgment that a wooden spade is better for agriculture than a modern tractor and the judgment which reverses this evaluation. And if I did accept Mr. Robinson's doctrine, I fear (although he regards this as irrelevant) that I should be less likely to resist the order of a tyrant bidding me to beat up the supposed enemies of my race or class. Whatever be the theory of it, I am as certain that cruelty is wrong as I am that grass is green or that two and two make four. If this certainty is merely contingent, then my whole universe is shaken. Mr. Robinson recommends his doctrine—I omitted this at an earlier stage—primarily on grounds of economy. But economy can be bought at too great a price if it means the obscuring of fundamental differences. The only justification of a philosophic theory is that it explains what it sets out to explain. My complaint against the emotive theory is that it does not explain moral goodness or moral actions or moral judgments. In spite of the ingenuity and candour of its authors all it does is to explain these things away.

III.—*By* R. C. Cross.

Mr. Robinson and Professor Paton differ sharply in the views they have put forward, but they have, I think, at least one very important point in common, namely their dissatisfaction, though perhaps in differing degree, with one type of ethical theory represented for example in such books as *The Right and The Good* and *Foundations of Ethics*. It may be convenient to have a short-hand term for referring to this type of theory, but in view of Professor Paton's protests against the usurpation of a respectable name, I hesitate to follow Mr. Robinson in calling it ethical objectivism, and shall call it instead ethical intuitionism, meaning thereby the same as Mr. Robinson means by ethical objectivism. Both Mr. Robinson and Professor Paton then are dissatisfied, though perhaps in differing degrees, with ethical intuitionism, and I have no wish to quarrel with them on this point. Various grounds for dissatisfaction are indicated in their papers—Mr. Robinson, for instance, thinks the theory, with its introduction of non-natural qualities, lacking in economy, and finds difficulty also with the sort of intuition involved ; and Professor Paton finds fault with its over-intellectualism. While agreeing with these criticisms I might add that the theory seems to me to set us off on a wrong track. Many ethical sentences have the same grammatical form as ordinary factual sentences, and the theory suggests that they therefore function logically in the same way ; that is to say, that just as a factual sentence like " there is meadowsweet in England " makes an assertion, and claims, in Mr. Robinson's phrase, to describe the world, so ethical sentences have a similar function. It also suggests, following from this, that evidence for or against ethical sentences is to be sought in a way at any rate analogous to that in which we seek evidence for or against ordinary factual assertions. It is true that the facts in the case of ethical sentences are of the peculiar kind described as non-natural. But still, they are there to be seen though the evidence in this case has to be obtained not with our physical sense organs but by some other form of " seeing." I think that the difficulties that consequently arise are due primarily to the initial move in assuming that ethical sentences do function in the same way as ordinary factual sentences, a point about which it may be possible to say a little later. It would not however be in place to spend time here considering the difficulties, or for that matter the important merits, of ethical intuitionism. Granted it has difficulties, Mr. Robinson has suggested an alternative which in various forms has gained considerable popularity in recent times, and has very considerable attractions. It is this theory that is up for discussion at the moment, and it is on it that I wish primarily to concentrate, though I hope to say a little incidentally about Professor Paton's counter-suggestions, and to add a few remarks of my own.

* * * * *

Professor Paton has already examined the emotive theory so exhaustively that I doubt if I can break any fresh ground. He has found serious difficulties in it, and I have some perplexities too, partly perhaps deriving from the same sources. Before I come to them however, I wish to say a word about the general method used in presenting the emotive theory. My trouble here may well be quite an imaginary one, but it is perhaps worth mentioning. When Professor Ayer argued for an emotive theory in *Language Truth and Logic* his procedure so far as it went was straightforward. When he came to deal with ethical judgments he had already satisfied himself that a sentence, to make sense, must be either a tautology or in principle verifiable in sense experience, and he had also explained the method of philosophical analysis which he was following. Thus when he came to deal with ethical sentences they had to fit in with this general background, and the obvious way to secure this was to adopt a straightforward psychological account. This, it will be recalled, Professor Ayer refused to do, because, as he said, " in our language sentences which contain normative ethical symbols are not equivalent to sentences which express psychological propositions." He thus reached the conclusion that ethical statements were unanalysable and therefore irreducible to any form of non-ethical statement ; and hence that their function was purely emotive. Clearly, however, more has to be done in the way of helping us to understand the functioning of ethical sentences ; and further, it would not, I think, be unfair to say that Professor Ayer reached the conclusions he did about ethical sentences as part of a general philosophical view in which other interests were stronger. Mr. Robinson however, and Professor Stevenson have not, explicitly at any rate, any special epistemological axes to grind. They advance the emotive theory on its merits. It is, however, at this point that my trouble begins, because in their expositions I find a certain difficulty over the general method they adopt to support their fundamental position that ethical judgments are emotive. We are, rather, simply told that they are so, or have to assume that they are so, and the fundamental position is left at that ; the rest is the working out of detail. To this it may very reasonably be replied that it is precisely in the successful working out in detail of the theory that the theory itself obtains its support. I am not entirely convinced by this reply, because of the difficulties I find in discovering ways of satisfying myself whether the detailed working out is being successful or not. Thus Professor Stevenson describes his method as that of ethical analysis, and he offers definitions of ethical terms. At first sight this seems reminiscent of the method of philosophical analysis we find in *Language Truth and Logic*, and suggests that these definitions will establish the theory in that they will show us how ethical terms can be defined in terms which are logically equivalent to them and reveal at the same time their emotive character. But quite obviously they will do no such thing, since it is clearly impossible to include the emotive element in the relation of logical equivalence. The best we can do about the emotive meaning, as both Professor Stevenson and Mr. Robinson say, is to " characterise " it. Thus we reach the " definition " offered by the first pattern of analysis, e.g., " this is wrong " means " I disapprove of this ; do so as well." But how can we satisfy ourselves that this is a successful " definition " or " characterisation " ? Indeed, if we look for a moment merely at the descriptive part, and if we think of logical equivalence, Professor Stevenson seems to be asserting a logical equivalence where Professor Ayer denied that there was any. So far as we keep to logical equivalence, it looks as though Professor Stevenson is constructing an artificial language, in which it will be a convention that " this is wrong " is logically equivalent to " I disapprove of this." But in any case, it is, on the view we are discussing, the emotive element in the ethical terms that is fundamental, and this is characterised in the present instance by the imperative element in the definition. There is no question here of any strict logical equivalence. At most the imperative " characterises " the emotive meaning. But granted that the " characterisation " is not based on a logical equivalence, by what other means can we recognise whether the " characterisation " is successful ? The simple answer would be that we should ask ourselves whether the characterisation satisfies our notions of what we mean when we ordinarily use the word. Here, however, Mr. Robinson raises an acute difficulty for us, since he insists that we are quite mistaken in what we ordinarily mean when we use ethical terms. He says, for example, on page 10 " I suggest that we are equally deceived in our use of the word " good " ; that we use it to mean an attribute entirely independent of minds, but there is no such attribute." Thus on this view we cannot judge the success or otherwise of the characterisations of ethical terms offered us by the emotive theory, by asking ourselves how far they seem satisfactorily to represent what we ordinarily mean by ethical terms. The characterisations, if they could be accepted, would display the emotive features of the ethical terms, and therefore support the emotive view. But the difficulty is to see on what grounds we ought to accept them. Perhaps it is some such point as this that Professor Paton has in mind when, on page 10, he speaks of " arguments based on what seem to be arbitrary definitions." I hope, therefore, if there is anything in what

I have said, that Mr. Robinson will explain further how the method of characterisation works; and meantime I have tried to indicate my difficulty about the general method of supporting the emotive theory, as opposed to the simple assertion that it is so.

* * * * *

Professor Stevenson and Mr. Robinson however clearly attach great importance, in supporting their theory, to the detailed investigation they make into the functioning of words in general, and it will be recalled that Mr Robinson begins his paper by seeking to establish the existence of independent emotive meaning as a prerequisite for the emotive theory, and then proceeds in the next stage to maintain that ethical words have independent emotive meaning. I wish now to look briefly at these two stages in his argument. First then, for independent emotive meaning. Mr. Robinson remarks that he has known at least one thinker who held that independent emotive meaning never occurs, though he is unable to report his reason, and he concludes by quoting Berkeley as sharing his own view that its occurrence is an obvious fact of experience. This is formidable, since I should shrink from being the other thinker who held that it never occurs. Indeed I am not clear that I do believe that it never occurs, but I should at any rate welcome further discussion, and content myself meantime with making a report; and as to Berkeley, I am encouraged by what is said later in the same section of the Principles " when a schoolman tells me ' Aristotle hath said it,' all I conceive he means by it is to dispose me to embrace his opinion with the deference and submission which custom has annexed to that name."

Mr Robinson uses two arguments in favour of independent emotive meaning. First he gives a list of pairs of words which he says " name the same thing but arouse different emotions towards it." Now let us take one of the pairs, say " nigger " and " negro." Mr Robinson says these name the same thing but arouse different emotions towards it. I assume, which appears unexceptionable, that these words are being used, let us say spoken by someone, and I report as follows : when the speaker says " negro " I understand him to be indicating a certain sort of human being with certain specific characteristics. When the speaker says " nigger " I understand him to be indicating as before, but I also infer something about his feelings, namely that *he* dislikes the object named. The word " nigger," however, does not function in the way of arousing *in me* a different emotion towards the object from that which the word " negro " does. So far as emotions are concerned, the only change that perhaps occurs is that I feel an emotion of dislike for the man who uses the word " nigger " instead of the word " negro " ; but that is clearly quite a different matter. Again, take another of Mr. Robinson's pairs, " to ape " and " to imitate." If the speaker—let us call him S—says " X imitates Mr. Churchill," I understand him to be representing or describing a certain mode of behaviour on the part of X. If, however, he says " X apes Mr. Churchill," I understand him to be describing roughly the same mode of behaviour on the part of X, but I also infer that he regards it with distaste. Now, particularly if S is a man for whose acumen I have high esteem, his disapproval of X, which I have inferred from his statement " X apes Mr. Churchill " may lead me to reconsider my views about X's conduct, and I may also in the end disapprove of X's conduct ; or alternatively my esteem of S may be such that now that I know he disapproves of X's conduct, I may simply on the strength of his authority do the same. In either case, however, it does not seem to be some peculiar power of the *word* " ape " in itself as used by S that directly arouses this disapproval. It should be noted that I am not saying that, for instance in the latter case, in saying " X apes Mr. Churchill " S is necessarily intending to assert anything about his own feelings ; we may say that S asserts or represents something about X, and expresses a certain feeling. This distinction between expressing and representing is of course familiar. It is put clearly for example by Carnap " we have here to distinguish two functions of language, which we may call the expressive function and the representative function. Almost all the conscious and unconscious movements of a person, including his linguistic utterances, express something of his feelings, his present mood, his temporary or permanent dispositions to reaction, and the like. Therefore we may take almost all his utterances and words as symptoms from which we can infer something about his feelings or his character. That is the expressive function portion of linguistic utterances (e.g. " this book is black ") as distinguished from other linguistic utterances and movements, has a second function : these utterances represent a certain state of affairs."[1] In this sense all words we speak are expressive, e.g. " the cat is black " at least expresses the occurrence of certain perceptual experiences. I am thus prepared to say that it is through the difference in the expressive function of the word " ape " as opposep to the word " imitate," that my emotion is changed ; but for the reasons explained I am not convinced that it is some emotive meaning attached to the word itself that directly works on my feelings and arouses the different emotion in me.

Mr. Robinson however has another argument to show the occurrence of independent emotive meaning—and he means by this, to recall his own words, " the power of a word to arouse emotion independently of what it describes or names." He appeals to interjections, and he is regarding them as words. Now let us take one of his own examples, " ouch." If I am fiddling with an electric iron which is not switched off, I may give myself an electric shock, and I may say " ouch." In saying " ouch " I am expressing a feeling of pain. But what is the response from the hearer who happens to be in the room with me ? I think an extremely common response is " what is the matter ? " or " did you give yourself a shock ?"; that is to say, the response is not, to use Professor Stevenson's phrase, " a range of emotions " at all. I think it is fair in what I have just been saying to pay attention primarily to the hearer,

---

[1] Philosophy and Logical Syntax, p. 23

since when we come to ethical sentences it is their independent emotive meaning as affecting the hearer, that is, on the emotive theory, particularly important. I conclude this discussion then with the feeling that Mr. Robinson's two arguments have not helped me as I had hoped in understanding the notion of independent emotive meaning. Yet of course the notion is fundamental to the theory we are discussing. For, to consider ethical words for a moment, we clearly do at times deliberately use ethical words not merely to vent or give expression to our feelings for our private satisfaction, but with a hearer in mind. In such cases, however, if we were to ignore the role played by emotive meaning in influencing the hearer it looks as though from the point of the hearer all we could be doing, on the general view we are discussing, would be simply telling him that we had a certain feeling. In that case, as Mr. Carritt has pointed out, the expressive theory would reduce to the more straightforward naturalist theory on which to say " X is wrong " would be simply to be telling the hearer that you disapproved of X; and the attendant difficulties of this simpler position, which the emotive theory as I understand it seeks to avoid, would arise.

Let us however assume that we do understand what is meant by independent emotive meaning, and pass to the second stage of Mr. Robinson's argument which is concerned now strictly with ethical words. Clearly, simply to say that these words are expressive would not do, since all words are expressive. In fact, as it will be remembered, this stage consists in the assertion that ethical words have independent emotive meaning. But on Mr. Robinson's own showing, so do many other words. Thus if the emotive theory is to be illuminating it seems not unreasonable to require it to tell us more about the particular set of feelings or attitudes with which the independent emotive meaning of ethical words is particularly concerned. Without this clue it is hard to see how we propose to distinguish ethical words from many others. This is a difficulty which appears to lurk in Mr. Robinson's own remark that " we cannot give a complete list of ethical words, or find an easy method of determining whether any given word is ethical ; but all we need do here is to list a few of them." Thus I agree with Professor Paton's complaint on page 3 that " we want to know precisely what it is that ethical language in its emotive use is supposed at once to express and to evoke." Mr. Robinson's view, as for instance on page 19, is presumably that ethical words evoke " the specifically moral emotions of approval and disapproval." But here again I agree with Professor Paton (page 3) that approval is " one of the vaguest words in the English language," and to describe ethical words as evoking " the specifically moral emotions " looks circular, unless there is some other way of identifying the moral emotions. Now it might be suggested that we are in fact all perfectly familiar with the " specifically moral emotions of approval and disapproval." Approval and disapproval are attitudes, among many other attitudes like " desire," " wish," and so on. We can give rough characterisations of these attitudes in the sort of way that is done by for example, Professor Stevenson in his article in *Mind* 1947, where he says of the moral use of the word " good," " this differs from the above (a non-moral use) in that it is about a different kind of interest. Instead of being about what the hearer or speaker *likes* it is about a stronger sort of approval—when a person *morally approves* of something, he experiences a rich feeling of security when it prospers, and is indignant or ' shocked ' when it doesn't." We could then go on to say that ethical words can be distinguished by being " about," to use Professor Stevenson's word, this special class of interests or attitudes which we can all easily recognise. The tendency then might be to make us, in Hume's Language, look within our bosoms ; and when we did so we would see a rich array of feelings and emotions, and above all of attitudes, which play such an important part in this type of theory. I am not suggesting that Mr. Robinson does tell us, or wish us, to do this. I am only saying that in the absence of further information about his usage of words like " emotion," " attitude," " approval," " disapproval," etc., we might be tempted to take this course. But if we did, we might find ourselves in almost as bad a plight as the critics of ethical intuitionism represent us to be in on that theory. They complain that on that theory we are invited so to speak to go digging aqout in the outside world trying to discover and identify non-natural qualities which we can't identify ; the present suggestion is that we should persevere in the digging process, only this time within our bosoms, and that in this case we shall be able to unearth and identify various attitudes, including the specifically moral attitudes. On this I can only report that my own endeavours are singularly unsatisfying. As Professor Findlay says in his article " Morality by Convention " in *Mind* 1944, " men have tended to operate with a picture of emotional life which has been, to an impossible degree, reduced and simplified. They have tended to picture emotions as " simple stirrings in men's bosoms " only accessible to an inward eye, and quite without any necessary relation to the objects in the environing world, or to the ways in which such objects lead us to behave. They have also tended to talk as if there were obvious surface marks by means of which the inward eye could recognise and classify these ' stirrings '." Thus granted that the emotive theory were to seek to distinguish ethical words by connecting their use with " the specifically moral emotions of approval and disapproval," it must try to illuminate the latter for us ; and an appeal to introspection is not, I suggest, likely to take us any distance.

Moreover, if we seek help from linguistic considerations I still think we can legitimately ask the emotive theory to say more than it normally does about the uses of words like " attitude," " approval," " disapproval," etc. For example, Professor Stevenson refrains from giving " a precise definition " of " attitude," and says it " must for the most part be understood from its current usage and from the usage of the many terms (" desire," " wish," " disapproval," etc.) which name specific attitudes."[2] But it seems to me that the " current usage " of most of these terms is vague in the extreme and stands badly in need of clari-

---

[2] Ethics and Language, p. 60

fication before the terms themselves could be helpful to us. Professor Findlay, in the article I have mentioned, recognises the need for such clarification when he sets out to discover the conditions which must be present before we are prepared to call some attitude an ethical one. It would not be appropriate to follow him further here ; the point I wish to make is that the emotive theory must, I think, help us more than it does, whatever the method adopted, in understanding its use of such key words as " approval," " moral emotion," etc. ; and I have suggested that an appeal to introspection, if that were intended, might lead to disappointment.

Professor Findlay's appeal, when on his method he is determining the conditions under which we should be prepared to call an attitude an ethical one, is to the objects of ethical reactions, which are, he considers, voluntary acts and agents. This reference to acts and agents is interesting because, to conclude this section with a more general point, it seems to me that a distinctive feature of at any rate an important group of the terms themselves which we classify as ethical—e.g., " right," " ought," etc.—is precisely their use in connection with action, with doing. Yet the curious thing, as Professor Paton has pointed out is that on the emotive theory it is descriptive meaning and not the emotive meaning so characteristic of ethical terms that is connected with action—in Professor Stevenson's words[3] " descriptive meaning is the disposition of a sign to affect cognition " and cognition in its turn (with certain qualifications) is " a disposition to actions." This is the more curious in that on the theory the emotive meaning which is the fundamental element in ethical terms is often characterised by the imperative form of words. But again it is not clear why the imperative form should be associated primarily with emotion. We certainly seem to use imperatives primarily with reference to action—a point on which I shall try to say a little more later.

* * * * *

---

[3] Ethics and Language, p. 67 and p. 63.

So far I have mainly tried to deal with some possible difficulties or obscurities within the emotive theory itself. On the other hand, what are the counter-suggestions available? The intuitionist theory in the form Mr. Robinson describes as " ethical objectivism " we have already agreed (for all its merits on certain points) to have special difficulties of its own. Professor Paton has made another suggestion, which I must leave to others to discuss in detail. I shall only observe that Professor Paton has I think still this at least in common with the ethical intuitionist, that he wishes to retain " true or false " as applicable to ethical judgments, though he is not accepting what the objectivist means by truth, but " extending the meaning of the word." He also agrees himself that there are great difficulties in establishing the sort of proposition he regards as fundamental " that morally good action must be willed as consistent with a law valid for others as well as ourselves " ; which I think he would hold to be a true synthetic a priori proposition. At any rate both he and the intuitionist are prepared in their diverse ways to show how we can establish the truth of some ethical sentences.

Now it will be recalled that at the beginning of this paper, in speaking of the ethical intuitionist, I expressed a doubt whether ethical sentences function in the same way as ordinary factual sentences. I wish therefore, if only for purposes of discussion, to conclude with the suggestion that their function is primarily imperatival, and that that is how we use them in ordinary life. Thus I agree with Professor Paton when he criticises Mr. Robinson's account of what we actually mean when we say, for example, " this act is right." I do not believe that we ordinarily mean anything like " this act has an utterly independent attribute of rightness." Instead, I want to say, borrowing a distinction of Professor Ryle's though possibly abusing it, that ethical sentences are connected with knowing how to act, and not with knowing that something is the case. So regarded ethical sentences naturally function in an imperatival way, for they are not describing facts about the world, but issuing instructions as to ways of acting, i.e. they are functioning as prescriptions or rules, and thus are outside the area of "knowing that" and of true and false. Sometimes I have thought, though I may be wrong, that Professor Paton comes near to such a view himself as when he remarks that "if we turn to practice, we have good grounds for adopting, and for recommending, principles which are necessary for successful achievement either in thought or in action, even although we may be unable to justify them otherwise."

At this point however we have to remember that the emotive theory also is prepared to see an imperatival element in ethical words—indeed the imperative is a way of bringing out the emotive meaning, as in, for example, Professor Stevenson's first pattern of analysis. Does this mean then that the view I am suggesting really falls back into an emotive theory? I do not intend this. Instead it seems to me that some imperatival modes of speech anyhow are primarily concerned with action, with issuing prescriptions as to how to do things, and not primarily with emotion. You will recall that as I pointed out earlier Professor Stevenson connects descriptive meaning with action, and emotive meaning, which in the first pattern he characterises by the imperative, with feeling. But the instructions for my vacuum cleaner say "Place bag, rim downwards, on a piece of paper, and while keeping the rim in firm contact with the paper, shake other end of bag by the tag provided." These instructions are imperatival in form; they tell me how to empty the bag; I can see no emotive effect in them—unless indeed their evocation of quite unintended despair. I suggest that the main division of meanings or uses of words into descriptive and emotive is far too simple and highly misleading. If we persist in it, we are likely to become involved in all sorts of difficulties, not only in the case of ethical sentences, but in the case of many other sentences too. We may find that there are many sentences which cannot be said in any plausible way to "describe" anything; and then we will be at a loss what to do with them—unless indeed, as in the present case with ethical sentences, we consign them to the vague limbo of "emotive utterances." I think that Berkeley himself, though Mr. Robinson has quoted him in support of the emotive theory, was aware of the complexities of the situation, when he said in the seventh Dialogue[4] " it seems to follow, that there may be another use of words besides that of marking and suggesting distinct ideas, to wit, the influencing our conduct and actions ; which may be done either by forming rules for us to act by, or by raising certain passions, dispositions, and emotions in our minds "—where it would surely be improper to ignore the " either "—" or." Moreover his example immediately following of the use of words like " agent " or " spirit " which he said, do not " stand for ideas " (nor presumably for emotions), and yet " are not insignificant neither," is deserving of attention.

Finally, if there is anything in what I have been saying it might be possible to hold that ethical utterances do not simply give vent to or arouse attitudes of approval or disapproval, which themselves are, to use Professor Paton's phrase " the product of merely contingent circumstances." It might be possible to hold this without involving ourselves alternatively in saying that they state truths or falsehoods. We might hold instead that our ethical utterances are rules or prescriptions for conduct, based on our own knowledge of how to act. And just as knowing how to act involves intelligence, and intelligent action is not a mere matter of chance, similarly the prescriptions we utter in this knowledge claim to exhibit intelligence, though there is no simple outside test of that intelligence, but it can only be tested by living out the rules themselves. However this may be I should certainly like to agree, if I knew how, with Professor Paton when he says " it seems to me obvious that intelligence (or stupidity) is manifested in actions and in practical judgments just as much as it is in theoretical judgments."

---

[4] Berkeley's Works, Ed. Fraser, Vol. II, p. 301.

WHAT CAN LOGIC DO FOR PHILOSOPHY?

Mr. K. R. Popper, Mr. W. C. Kneale and Professor A. J. Ayer.

I.—*By* K. R. Popper.

The aim of this paper is to show, with the help of a few examples, that certain very simple logical considerations can throw some light upon philosophical problems, including some of the traditional problems of metaphysics and theology. One of my main points will be to establish by way of these examples, that there are such things as philosophical problems—not only pseudo-problems. Another point will be that we may apply to them simple methods of logical analysis which have little or nothing to do with an analysis in terms of our elementary experiences (sense-data, perceptions, or what not) or with an analysis of the meaning of words. The methods I have in mind are, rather, those of constructing, or analysing, or criticizing, arguments, and ways of approaching the problem.

One of my main difficulties in preparing this paper was that of selecting my examples, that is, of selecting philosophical problems ; especially in view of the fact that the most obvious and important source of examples—the philosophy of language—is one which is to be discussed in another symposium, and therefore better left aside. I have tried hard to select examples which I think are both representative and interesting ; but I fear that I have not quite succeeded. I thought, further, that since in a short paper like this it is impossible to go very deeply into the analysis of any one problem, it will be better to select a number from various representative fields, including what is usually called metaphysics and ethics, and to be frankly sketchy. On the other hand, I have tried to introduce at least some slight degree of coherence into my somewhat mixed collection of problems which ranges from the problem of the existence of philosophy and the problems of causality and determinism to those of the role of experience in ethics.

1.

Let us begin with a brief discussion of an extremely general philosophical problem—the much discussed question whether there is anything which may be called " philosophy."

I have always felt much sympathy with Kant, the positivists and all others who, repelled by the extravagant claims of some philosophical system builders, began to doubt whether there was anything at all in philosophy. I have only admiration for those who reacted against apriorism—the attitude of possessing, if not all fundamental knowledge, at least the key to it—and against empty verbalism. But it is interesting to observe the fate of these brave fighters against apriorism and against verbalism.

The positivists who were mainly anti-apriorists, that is to say, those who believed that there is no room for a third realm of studies besides the empirical sciences on the one hand and knowledge of logic and mathematics on the other, found themselves nearly immediately in difficulties when asked to give a criterion of empirical knowledge. Their answers were, very often, naive and mistaken. But this is not my main point here. What was so striking was what I may call a strong aprioristic character of their answers. Their attempts to characterise empirical knowledge led them to the construction of fairly complicated philosophical systems, such as the sense-data theories or phenomenalism—systems which were perhaps not so very different from those against which they originally reacted. And these systems, in spite of paying lip-service to anti-apriorism, took up more and more the strange character of the old aprioristic systems ; one felt quite clearly that their defenders had an axe to grind, and that they were much more interested in this philosophical axe-grinding than in learning from experience.

A similar fate befell those positivists who reacted not so much against philosophical apriorism but rather against philosophical verbalism. To them, philosophy was " mere words "—meaningless verbiage. But when confronted with the task to explain the criterion of meaningful language, as opposed to meaningless verbiage, they got into very serious difficulties, proposing, for example, criteria in terms which turned out to be themselves meaningless. They discovered that they had started from a naive philosophy of language ; and they were soon surrounded by difficulties which they found practically unsurmountable. To these difficulties they reacted by giving up arguing about problems ; instead, these philosophers, who had started by denouncing philosophy as merely verbal, and who had demanded that, instead of attempting to solve them, we should turn away from the verbal problems to those which are real and empirical, found themselves bogged up in the thankless and apparently endless task of analysing and unmasking verbal pseudo problems.

This is how I see the recent history of a movement with which I thoroughly sympathise, as far as its starting points are concerned—the revolt against apriorism and philosophical verbiage. It has shown, I believe, that there exist, at the very least, two kinds of philosophical problems—the philosophy of the empirical sciences, which tries to analyse what makes the empirical sciences empirical, and the philosophy of language, including the theory of meaning.

But where does logic come in here ?

The parallelism in the fate of the two revolts, against apriorism and against verbiage, does not seem to be accidental. And I believe that the development could have been, to a certain extent, foreseen. The reason is that an assertion like " there cannot exist statements besides those of the natural sciences and of logic," is very similar to the paradox of the liar, since it is certainly no statement of the natural sciences, and hardly one of logic (since it is about logic). Thus one way in which logic, and especially the analysis of paradoxes, might help us is by warning us against such sweeping aprioristic assertions and positions, and by making us a little more modest.

2.

But does this mean that there must be a " science of philosophy " or a philosophical system ? I do not know, and I think rather not.

I believe that most of us think too much in terms of subject-matters or disciplines—physics, chemistry, biology, etc. Admittedly, we have in some of these unified theoretical systems. But these may or may not be found. In any case, we find them in our attempts, not so much to build up a coherent " body of knowledge " (a particularly silly expression), but to solve certain definite problems. Our subject matters or disciplines or " bodies of knowledge " are, I think, largely didactic devices designed to help in the organisation of teaching. The scientist—the man who does not only teach but adds to our knowledge—is, I believe, fundamentally a *student of problems*, not of subject matters.

Now problems often cut through all these subject matters. A problem of neuro-physiology, for example, may need, for its solution, bits from practically all the sciences known to us. And the fact that it needs mathematics, for its solution does not make it a mathematical problem or one of physics.

From this point of view, there is no particular difficulty in admitting the existence of philosophical problems. They may turn up in all sorts of contexts, and may need all sorts of considerations—empirical, logical, mathematical—for their solution. They can be called " philosophical " either because of certain historical associations, or because of the fact that they are of a *second-storey character*—connected with questions *about* science, or *about* mathematics, or *about* art, etc.

There seems to be *one* great difficulty to this view, from the point of view of those anti-aprioristic tendencies which I share : how do we *test* an answer to a philosophical problem ? An answer to a scientific problem, it seems, can be tested by experience ; but what about the status of an answer which is neither purely logical nor testable by empirical science ?

The proper reply to this is, I suppose, on the following lines : philosophical answers must always remain tentative. There is no reason, it seems, why we should reach agreement on them. But this is no reason to deny the existence of philosophical problems. It is an aprioristic dogma (held by some positivists) that only such problems are real problems to which we can (" in principle ") find a definite, established answer. This dogma must be given up. Even in the empirical sciences, our answers are, as a rule, tentative. They have in the past often changed, and we cannot know whether in future they will not continue to do so. Admittedly, the situation in philosophy is worse, owing to the absence of empirical tests, and those who find this situation distressing should better turn to some other field. Nevertheless, we sometimes make some progress—for example, we may discover that some progress—for example, we may discover that some proposed theory does not really answer the question which it is supposed to answer. This may not be much of a success, but it is something ; and it is the kind of thing which is achieved, mainly, with the help of logic.

3.

I shall turn to the philosophy of philosophy at the end of this paper. Meanwhile I intended to discuss a series of slightly more concrete problems ; and I take as my first example the problem of *causality*, because it is an example of a problem where logical analysis can help us even in a mildly constructive way.

In this section, I shall sketch[1] an analysis of what may be called the logical mechanism of causal explanation ; and I shall apply the analysis to some questions raised by Hume, and by some theists.

A scientific explanation of a certain singular event E (i.e. an event that happens in a certain place at a certain time) always consists of a number of statements from which a

---

[1] Cp my *Logik der Forschung*, section 12, pp. 26ff ; *The Poverty of Historicism* III (*Economica*, N.S. XII), section 28, pp. 75f, and *The Open Society* II, note 9 to ch. 25.

singular statement e, describing the event E, can be deduced. These premises or explanatory statements are of two kinds, universal statements u (or laws), and singular statements i which state what may be called the initial conditions.

In other words, an explanation of an event E consists of a deductive inference,

$$\frac{\begin{array}{c}u\\i\end{array}}{e}$$

in which from universal laws u and initial conditions i the statement e describing the event E (which is to be explained) is deduced.

Trivial premises are, of course, often taken for granted, or " suppressed."

In order that the explanation should be acceptable or satisfactory, the statements u and i must be well tested (*independently* of the event E in question ; see below).

In the natural sciences, we usually do not use any longer the vague terms " cause " and " effect " ; but I shall now show that the logical mechanism just analysed can be interpreted as covering what may be called a " causal explanation," and that what is usually called " cause " is described, in a causal explanation, by the initial conditions i, and the " effect " by e.

Take, as an example, that the event E which we wish to explain causally is the death of Mr. X. Somebody may suggest that the cause of his death is that he took a spoonful of potassium cyanide ; and if we can find evidence that he did, we shall accept this as " cause " of his death. But why ? We may also find that he ate, immediately before, a bar of chocolate. Why do we say that his taking potassium cyanide caused his death rather than his taking chocolate ? Obviously because we assume the truth of the universal law that everybody who takes a spoonful of potassium cyanide dies at once, while we do not believe that a corresponding law holds for bars of chocolate. In other words, we accept the suggested cause only because we believe in the truth of a certain universal law u (" Everybody who takes a spoonful of potassium cyanide dies at once "), which, together with the description of the cause, i.e., with the initial condition i (" Mr. X took a spoonful of potassium cyanide "), allows us to deduce the statement e (" Mr. X. died ") which describes the effect which is to be explained.

A fairly important point in our analysis is that we must have good evidence in favour of u and i, *independently* of the fact that e is true ; that is to say, u and i must be well tested, and we must not count the fact that X died after taking potassium cyanide as evidence in favour of u, nor the fact that u and e are established as evidence in favour of i.

I do not, of course, believe that this simple analysis is exhaustive. Undoubtedly there are cases which conform to our analysis but which we should hesitate to call causal explanations. For example, the famous syllogism " All men are mortal. Socrates is a man. Socrates is mortal " conforms to our scheme. Nevertheless, it is certainly a bit awkward to say that the fact that Socrates is a man is the cause of his being mortal. And we should be even more reluctant to call a certain day the cause of the following night, even though we believe in the truth of the universal law which allows us to deduce (or predict) the arrival of the particular night in question from the statement that it was daytime. I believe that it is possible to augment our analysis in such a way as to allow for the difference between such cases of deductive explanations or predictions and the other cases which we may feel inclined to accept as truly causal explanations. But I shall not go into this matter here. For our present purposes it is sufficient to note that all causal explanations fall under our scheme, even though other things may fall under our scheme as well. In fact, all that we need at present is this :

If anybody says that a certain singular event I is the cause of a certain singular event E, then he tacitly assumes that there is an independently testable universal law u such that from u and i (i.e. the statement describing I) we can deduce e (the statement describing e). Or more briefly, to say that I is the cause of E is to assume the truth of a universal law u such that, in its presence, e follows from i.

To be sure, in most cases of ordinary experience, u is " suppressed," that is to say, u is taken to be so trivial that we do not mention it. For example, if we say that my holding a match to it was the cause of this fire's beginning to burn, or when we say that the cause of the death of Charles I was that his head had been cut off, then we are, as a rule, not conscious of the fact that we assumed, in each case, the truth of a universal law. But if we had reason to believe that people whose heads had been cut off usually are the better for this operation, then we certainly should not accept the explanation which historians offer for the death of Charles I.

All this is very trivial ; but it can throw some light on well known philosophical problems.

Let us first take Hume's problem whether there is a *necessary* connection between a cause and the effect which it produces. Hume's answer is negative. Ours, I think, must be affirmative.

It must be affirmative because whenever we consider I to be the cause of E, we do so in view of a (usually suppressed) law u in the presence of which e *follows* from i ; and since we may take it that the relationship of deducibility may be described as a " necessary " one, we may say that the connection between I and E is a necessary one (although not " absolutely necessary," but only " necessary relative to u.")

Hume sees only I and E, and overlooking the suppressed u, he thinks that there is no connection between them— nothing beyond the fact that events similar to I have been, as a rule, followed by events similar to E. He does not notice that, if we formulate this fact in form of a universal law, the dependence of E upon I becomes, relative to this law, logically necessary. And he does not see that, even if we introduce the universal law in question merely as a tentative hypothesis, this means that we assume—tentatively and hypothetically—that the relationship between I and E is a necessary one, in the sense described.

I shall not here discuss Hume's attempt causally to explain a belief in a regularity or law by habit, although I think that this particular attempt at causally explaining away causality can be easily shown to be completely mistaken ; I only wish to point out that he overlooked that a belief in a universal law *u*—whether or not causally explicable in terms of habits or associations—is, rationally, identical with a belief in a *necessary* connection between the corresponding *I*'s and *E*'s. We need not believe in the necessity or even in the truth of *u* in order to see that, given *u*, *e* can be logically obtained from *i*. Accordingly, we may describe the situation in this way : in the same degree in which we believe in *u* or doubt *u* or disbelieve in *u*, in the same degree do we believe or doubt or disbelieve that there holds a kind of *necessary* connection between *I* and *E*—a connection such that, given *I*, *E must* follow.

Our simple and somewhat trivial logical analysis thus allows us to explain certain psychological attitudes, and it does so perhaps better than the psychological analysis employed by Hume.

A second application of our analysis is to the cosmological proof of the existence of God (Aquina's " Second Way.") This argument has often been criticised, from many points of view, and it has recently been reformulated by Whittaker. It seems to be based on the intuitive idea that, if we can ask for the cause of an event, we can also ask for the cause of this cause. In this way we obtain a regressive chain of causes, and, if the regress is to be finite, a first cause, which we may call " God " ; or more precisely (since a cause is not a person or thing but an event or fact), the fact of the existence of God.

I shall not discuss that aspect of this argument which I consider the only one which is philosophically relevant (viz., that this argument, even if successful, could at best prove the existence of a powerful Creator, while what interests us is the existence of a God who is good). I shall only point out that the regress from one " cause " to a preceding one is always relative to one or another *universal law*, and that, accordingly, the argument from causation assumes the universal laws of nature to be given. It therefore cannot conceive God as the creator of universal laws, or of order in nature, and must clash with the design argument (St.

Thomas's " Fifth Way "), especially in the form proffered by Jeans and Whittaker (in which the fact that some natural laws can be conveniently formulated in a mathematical language is taken to indicate that God must be a mathematician).

4.

I now turn to the problem of determinism. It is easy enough to visualise the world in the way the determinist sees it—as a kind of clockwork or planetary system or as an electro-chemical machine. It is more difficult to analyse in words the determinist's faith.

I think the following formulation may be satisfactory.

Every future event, the determinist may say, can be predicted with any desired degree of precision, provided we can measure all the relevant initial conditions (with an appropriate degree of precision), and provided we have completed the discovery of the relevant natural laws.

According to quantum mechanics, this statement is either not relevant or not true; but I shall neglect this aspect. Even without quantum mechanics, we can see that the statement is very unsatisfactory. Any more complicated and more distant event will defeat us; we simply cannot obtain the knowledge of the initial conditions which we would need; and we even cannot, as a rule, find out, from the formulation of the problem—the event to be predicted—what the initial conditions are which will be relevant to the problem, and to which degree of exactness they must be known. (The only exception to this seems to be that misleading case, the planetary system—a simple mechanism which is as well insulated as a clockwork, and not at all characteristic of the physical world in general). Thus we shall probably never be able to predict the weather in London with any precision even for a month ahead.

But apart from the very important and insurmountable difficulties which are connected with he initial conditions, there is no reason to believe that we shall ever have a complete knowledge of the universal laws of nature. We operate with hypotheses, and we find again and again that we have to improve upon them. And even if this process would come to an end, we could not know that it has come to an end.

Thus the determinist's programme is, at best, a pious wish, for a kind of divine omniscience; but it may be something worse—a completely misleading idea. (This is suggested by two aspects of scientific method which, it appears, is always one of bold oversimplifications. We have reason to believe, first that most of our so-called natural laws are lucky oversimplifying guesses; secondly that our experimental method involves interference with the things we study: we construct artificial, oversimplified cases—cases for study. One may even put it, perhaps, like this: the natural sciences do not deal so much with hard facts as with *interpretations* of facts, in the light of our theories, guesses, prejudices).

This discussion of determinism is completely independent of any problem of ethics. But it may clear the ground for one simple logical consideration in the field of ethics.

I shall discuss the question:

When do people consider human behaviour as praiseworthy or blameworthy action and when do they consider it not so?

I suggest a rough and very simple answer:

If people believe that under the same initial conditions, *as far as they can be independently ascertained or tested*, all or most people would act in this way, in other words, if they think that the behaviour can be satisfactorily (i.e., without the help of *ad hoc* hypotheses)*causally explained* with the help of independently established initial conditions and universal laws ("All men—or most men—in such circumstances act in this way"), then they do not think that it is either praiseworthy or blameworthy. Or in other words, they think it praiseworthy or blameworthy or, as we may say, "morally free," to the degree in which it is not causally explicable, on independently ascertainable initial conditions. They may then say, if they are determinists, that the action flows from the personality or from early influences, etc.; that is to say, they postulate hidden initial conditions. Or they may say if they are indeterminists, that the action was due to the free will of the individual. But both agree, roughly, that if ascertainable initial conditions—those for which we can obtain independent evidence—can be considered as sufficient " causes," and to the degree to which they can be so considered, the action is not one to be morally judged.

This is just another suggestion about the way in which our very simple scheme of causal explanation may contribute a little towards certain philosophical problems.

5.

Our analysis of causal explanation can be applied to other and, in my opinion, more important problems—to problems of the philosophy of society, and of history. I have more especially, one problem in mind——the problem whether there are what may be called " natural laws of social life " or " sociological laws " ; that is to say, laws which describe regularities of social life which are not produced by legislation, or by religious or moral custom.

The problem mentioned is, of course, of fundamental interest for the student of the methods of the social sciences. Nevertheless, it is not merely a methodological problem. It is of great significance for our whole attitude towards society and politics. We enter, as it were, into a new world—the world of purposes, of rational actions which pursue ends, and, of course, of irrational actions also. Has this world a similar structure as the world of physics and, say, physiology ? The question is certainly of philosophical interest, even if it turns out to be a simple question of empirical fact. But it hardly is a question of empirical fact : at least it is not one on which social scientists have reached agreement. (Even in the natural sciences, we are constantly dealing with *interpretations*, rather than with hard facts. In the social sciences, this seems to be so to a higher degree).

The question whether there exist sociological laws has often been answered, both in the affirmative and in the negative, in a way which I consider mistaken. People have asserted, for example, that there are laws of social evolution. I do not think that there are good reasons to believe that such laws exist, either in the field studied by biology or in that of sociology. Others have denied the existence of sociological laws altogether, the field of economics included. (This would make practically all rational political action impossible, since it does make impossible to predict the consequences of changed conditions). Many people seem still to believe in the view of Comte, and Mill—that there are two kinds of laws, " laws of succession " (or of evolution) and " laws of co-existence."

I think that nearly all these views are mistaken and mainly because of misunderstandings of a logical character.

It is impossible for me here to go into these interesting questions of social philosophy in detail, and unnecessary because I have done so elsewhere[2]. I shall confine myself to a story : A friend of mine, an economist, recently expressed his scepticism concerning his science. In his opinion, economic laws did not exist. Economics was only a system of empty definitions, without empirical content. He illustrated this by an example. " If asked by the Government what policy they should adopt in order to have full employment without inflation, I could not answer ; indeed, I suspect, that there is no answer." I pointed out to him that he had, in order to illustrate the absence of economic laws, just formulated one : The statement " There does not exist a policy which allows us to have full employment without inflation " (whether this is true is another question) is indeed a model of a sociological law. In order to see this clearly, we have only to apply some of the simplest logical rules to it—the equivalence of universal statements to negated existential ones. On the basis of this equivalence, all universal laws can be expressed in " There-does-not-exist " form. For example, the second law of thermodynamics by " There does not exist a machine which is one hundred per cent efficient." The similarity with the economic hypothesis mentioned above is obvious."

---

[2] Cp. especially my *Poverty of Historicism* (*Economica* N.S. XI and XIII).

6.

Another example of the significance of logic for ethics.

Perhaps the simplest and the most important point about ethics is purely logical. I mean the impossibility to derive non-tautological ethical rules—imperatives : principles of policy ; aims ; or however we may describe them—from statements of facts.

Only if this fundamental logical position is realised can we begin to formulate the real problems of moral philosophy, and to appreciate their difficulty.

As one of the most central problems of the theory of ethics, I consider the following : If ethical rules (aims, principles of policy, etc.) cannot be derived from facts—how then can we explain that we can learn about these matters from experience ?

We can also put the question in this way : if aims cannot be derived from facts, can we do more than see that our system of aims is coherent ? And if it is, can we do more than try to alter the facts, to " reform " them—in such a way that they conform to our aims ?

The simple answer is, I believe, that not all the facts which can be altered can be altered in conformity with every preconceived and internally coherent system of aims. To take the example mentioned above. We may know that certain facts—such as unemployment, or inflation—can be altered. We may aim, on moral grounds, to avoid both. But we may learn from our attempt to do so that our system of aims, although internally coherent, does not cohere with some of the laws of economics, previously unknown to us.

7.

To close with a general remark.

A number of philosophical problems can be shown, it appears, to be composed of an empirical and of a logical component. The analysis into these components, together with the claim that there is no further problem left, do not, if successful, establish that the original problem was a pseudo problem ; on the contrary, it shows that there is a problem, and the way in which it can be solved.

By WILLIAM KNEALE.

(1)

I AGREE with nearly all that Dr. Popper has said, but I think a hostile critic might object that he has not explained what he means by " logic " or tried to say in general terms how logic can be of service to philosophy. No doubt he can make a good reply to this charge. For he has stated his views on the nature of logic very clearly in a number of recent articles, and he may argue that it is more important for his present purpose to give a number of examples of the use of logic from which we may learn the " feel " of certain kinds of problems. It seems to me, nevertheless, that it may be useful to approach the subject of our symposium in a more direct way, namely, by considering the attitude which philosophers have adopted towards logic and the attitude which they should adopt.

When Aristotle introduced Logic into the household of Philosophy, he did not suggest that she should be received as a member of the family, and she was not treated as such, in spite of a plea from her admirer Chrysippus. On the contrary, until last century she remained a mere maid of all work, required to do everything for the family, including some tasks that were beyond her strength. But at the end of last century she obtained a position of greater independence and dignity as housekeeper to Mathematics, and since that time her relation to Philosophy has been obscure. Mr. Russell maintains that, if she is asked, she will still visit the house of Philosophy from time to time in order to do for her old mistress as a kind of intellectual charwoman. On the other hand, some of her new friends, including Professor Ayer, say she is so angry about her treatment in the past by Metaphysics, the eldest son of the family, that she has already done for him in another sense of that phrase. Dr. Popper refuses to believe this story, saying that she could never behave so violently. Whatever the truth of the matter may be, Metaphysics has not been seen about lately, and Philosophy is still wondering what she may expect from Logic. Now I want to suggest that, if Philosophy is wise, she will admit Logic as a full member of her family, not so much in the hope of getting some odd favours for the other members as in order to set right an old wrong and increase her own reputation with persons of good judgement. For, in spite of the obscurity of her status, Logic has won for herself the respect of the scientific world.

In plain English, my suggestion is that philosophers should not spend so much time debating the boundaries of their subject and the propriety of their methods, but recognize that in logic they have at least one genuine field of study where intensive work may yield rich rewards. In recent years a great deal of the most valuable work on logic has been done by mathematicians. To put things on the lowest level, it is a pity that all the kudos should go to persons of another profession. But if that were the only consideration, I should not be much concerned. For demarcation disputes between scientific trade unions are of no great importance. If mathematicians are ready to take over some work that philosophers persist in neglecting, good luck to them ! In the long run all who are interested in the work will call themselves mathematicians, and that name will come to have a slightly wider application that it does at present. My chief reason for hoping that logic will be taken more seriously in philosophical studies is a belief that some of the most important questions of logic are philosophical rather than mathematical according to the present usage of these words and that persons with a philosophical type of mind should find them interesting. I do not want to enter here on a discussion of the meaning of the word " philosophical ", and so I shall try to explain what I have in mind by means of two examples. If my belief is correct, you will recognize why I have chosen them.

Let us consider the foundations first. Logic has been defined in various ways, but it seems most satisfactory to begin by saying that it is the theory of entailment, *i.e.*, the study of what follows from what and why. There are reasons for holding that this definition is too wide, but at first sight it is more likely to seem too narrow. Since we often say that one proposition follows from another in virtue of the logical forms of the two propositions and sometimes talk about logical form without explicit reference to entailment, it may be thought that logic should be defined by reference to form rather than to entailment. But how are we to understand the phrase " logical form " ? If we talk about the shape of negative, conjunctive, disjunctive, conditional, universal and existential statements in a particular language, *e.g.*, ordinary English or Peano's symbolism, we seem to be tying ourselves to the study of that language in a way which is not proper for logicians. For logic is surely not concerned with English to the exclusion of French, or with Peano's symbolism to the exclusion of Hilbert's. Nor is it enough to say that a negative statement is any statement which is equivalent to an English statement containing " not ". For that still leaves us tied to English as the standard language. The only way out of this difficulty is to define the logical forms by reference to entailment. This is what Dr. Popper has done recently in detail.[1] We may say, for example, that a statement a has the logical force of a conjunction of b and c if, and only if, b and c together entail a and a entails b and a entails c. I do not mean that the use of the word " entails " or any synonym is essential. But other methods have the same effect. Thus, if we define a non-general truth-function by means of a truth-table such as the following :

b	c	conj. (b, c)
T	T	T
T	F	F
F	T	F
F	F	F

we are really specifying certain relations between the conditions for the truth of the truth-function and the

---

[1] Cf. his article " New Functions for Logic " in *Mind*, vol. LVI, 1947.

conditions for the truth of some other statements, called its arguments. The table printed here is just another way of saying what I have said above by the use of " entails ".

Now, as Dr. Popper has shown, the only *technical* terms we need for formulating logic in this fashion (at least up to and including the restricted calculus of propositional functions) are " entails " and a phrase such as " the result of substituting x for y in z ". But this is not to say that we need no other terms whatsoever. On the contrary, the presentation of logic as a meta-linguistic theory involves the use of a number of words that are sometimes called logical (*e.g.*, " and ", " if ", " all ") or symbolic devices that play the same role ; my example shows this clearly enough. There is no vicious circularity, however, in such use. For when we propose to speak about the logic of a certain language or class of languages (*i.e.*, about the rules of entailment holding for that language or those languages), we are entitled to talk in a language that shares some features with the languages we talk about. But some interesting questions arise. What is the minimum apparatus required in a meta-language for talking about the logic of a given language ? And if we cannot talk about the logic of a language L, without using a language L_2 which itself has a logic formulable in another language L_3, what bearing has this on the thesis of those who call themselves conventionalists ? Since our deliberate conventions must always be formulated in some natural language, can we ever by convention escape to anything radically new ? Finally, what sort of truth are we enunciating when we talk about the need for a hierarchy of languages ? I do not think that all these questions have been answered satisfactorily so far, and they seem to me to be questions that should interest philosophers for their own sake. But if they have been answered satisfactorily, there remains at least a lot to be done before the answers are as widely appreciated as they should be, and this appears to be work for philosophers.

For our second example let us consider the essential incompleteness of any deductive system of more than a certain richness in types of variable. Gödel has shown that, if a formalized system like that of *Principia Mathematica* is at once self-consistent and rich enough to contain the natural numbers or to allow for their introduction by definition, it is possible to construct in the symbolism of the system formulæ which cannot be demonstrated or refuted within the system, although they are necessarily true or necessarily false, as the case may be.[2] In order to decide whether such a formula is true or false, it is necessary to use a system that includes not only the symbolic apparatus of that with which we started, but also variables of a higher type than any found in the original system. And when we have succeeded in reaching a decision in this way, we find that it is possible to construct formulæ which cannot be decided in our new system. And so on *ad infinitum*. In short, the realm of logically necessary truths cannot be exhausted by any axiomatized system, however rich. Starting from a different point and working independently, Tarski has proved a similar conclusion, namely, that we shall inevitably fall into self-contradiction if we try to define within a formalized language what it is for any formula of that language to be true.[3]

These results seem surprising because we find it difficult to reconcile the story of the inexhaustible wealth of logic with the simplicity of its beginnings. Like Locke, we are all inclined to suppose that logic is trivial. And so in a sense it is ; for the most complicated demonstration is only a sequence of obvious steps. But we fall into error because we overlook the increase of complexity comes with ever higher types of variables. Logic is not all like the so-called algebra of logic, that is to say, the algebra which can be interpreted either as a calculus of classes or as a calculus of propositions. For there is no rule of thumb by which all formulæ constructed with logical symbolism alone can be resolved into patent truisms or patent contradictions. Here again we have something that should be of the greatest

---

[2] " Über formal unentscheidbare Sätze der Principia Mathematica und verwandter Systeme " in *Monatshefte für Mathematik und Physik*, vol. XXXVIII, 1931.

[3] " Der Wahrheits-begriff in dem förmalisierten Sprachen " in *Studia Philosophica*, vol. I, 1936.

interest to philosophers. I do not say that it is our duty to try to turn ourselves into mathematicians in order that we may take part in the progress of mathematics. But it is surely our business to try to understand what happens during the advance. For one at least of the marks of a philosophical mind is a desire to make the truth seem plausible, and the work that philosophers can do by following up this interest of theirs may be of great importance to civilization.

(2)

Although I have been arguing that philosophers should cultivate logic for its own sake, I wish also to maintain that the rest of their work will profit from this study, and that in an obvious way.

Whatever we may say about the nature of philosophy, we must admit that during our philosophizing we often have occasion to use technical terms of logic. When, for example, we discuss phenomenalism, we talk a lot about hypothetical propositions. And in our inquiries about induction we try to distinguish different kinds of universal propositions. This frequent use of logical terminology is not surprising. For it is obvious that the testing of philosophical suggestions involves saying " What would follow if this were true? " Socrates could do this without using much technical terminology, and so, no doubt, could we if we tried hard. But when once we have come to understand what we are about, it is natural and time-saving to use the language of logic. There is also another and more important reason for the use of such language by philosophers. We are interested in the classification of the various claims men make to knowledge, and before we have gone very far in this enterprise we discover that we must take account of the logical forms of the assertions in which they express these claims. It is of great importance, for example, that the statement " Iron is magnetic " is universal. If a man really knows that iron is magnetic, his knowledge of this must be something very different from his knowledge that the canister holding his tobacco is made of iron. Now confusion and frustration may result if philosophers use logical terminology without paying much attention to the development of logic. Natural scientists often accuse us of being a generation or more out of date in our references to science, and it does sometimes seem that metaphysics is the heaven to which good hypotheses go when they die. But it is just as serious if philosophers persist in using logical doctrines that are discredited. I shall try to illustrate this by means of an example.

There are still some philosophers who try to work with Kant's definition of an analytic judgment as one in which the predicate concept is contained in the subject concept, although not all judgments have subjects and predicates and none of those that do are of a kind we want to call analytic. But this confusion is now well known and requires no further comment. It is less widely recognized, however, that it is unprofitable to define an analytic proposition as one guaranteed by the law of non-contradiction alone. According to the generally received tradition all logical truisms are to be accounted analytic, but it is not the case that all logical truisms can be shown to be such simply by presentation in the form " Not both p and not p ", *i.e.*, without appeal to any other principle than the law of non-contradiction. Let us consider, for example, the conditional statement " If all animals are mortal and all men are animals, then all men are mortal ". This is a statement such as Aristotle might have used for illustrating the principle of the syllogism in *Barbara*, and it is a logical truism. But it is not obviously of the form " Not both p and not p ". It is true that we can derive a self-contradiction from its negative, but to do so we must use the principle of the syllogism in *Barbara* as a rule of inference. Now those who accept the definition of " analytic " mentioned above and hold at the same time that all logical truisms are analytic seem to be saying in effect that all logical truisms can be derived from " Not both p and not p " by substitution of other expressions for " p ", or, to put the matter in a more striking way, that with substitution as our sole procedure of inference and " Not both p and not p " as our sole axiom we can obtain the whole of logic. And this is false.

M

If we wish to use the word "analytic" in such a way that all logical truisms are analytic, it seems best to define the word by reference to logic. This is what Mr. Russell does in the preface to the second edition of his *Philosophy of Leibniz*, published in 1937. He writes there: "The important distinction is between propositions deducible from logic and propositions not so deducible; the former may advantageously be defined as *analytic*, the latter as *synthetic*". This is undoubtedly an improvement on most earlier definitions, but it should be noticed that we cannot use this definition unless we are already able to recognize propositions deducible from logic. And so we explain nothing if we now say that all logical truisms are analytic; for we only assert the triviality that they follow from themselves. In order to characterize logic we must proceed in some other way. Now it is often said that logical truisms are statements whose truth is guaranteed by the rules of usage of the symbols they contain. This description undoubtedly includes all truisms that beong to logic, but it may conceivably include others; for it is equivalent to the old phrase "*a priori*", and some philosophers have maintained that there are *a priori* truths other than those commonly assigned to logic. If in order to be more precise we suggest that logic is concerned only with truisms whose truth is guaranteed by the rules of usage for the *formative* signs alone (*i.e.*, the signs definable by reference to entailment in the way adopted by Dr. Popper), then there are undoubtedly *a priori* truths other than those of logic, *e.g.*, "Cats are animals". And if we combine this view of logic with the usage of "analytic" suggested by Mr. Russell in the passage I have quoted, we come to the conclusion that there are synthetic *a priori* truths. Why does this conclusion appear shocking? Is it not because the words "analytic" and "synthetic" have come to have overtones of meaning (dare I say "emotive meaning") which are relatively independent of any precise definitions we may offer? If my diagnosis is correct, it is time that these words were banished from philosophical discussions. When we are no longer worried by associations with Kantianism on the one

WHAT CAN LOGIC DO FOR PHILOSOPHY? 163

hand and Positivism on the other, we may be able to think about these matters more clearly.

(3)

I shall not try to add any more to the detailed illustrations that Dr. Popper has given in support of his thesis that logic can help in the solution of philosophical problems, because I do not want to side-track the discussion by starting a lot of disconnected controversies. But the points of detail he has raised are interesting in themselves, and it is proper that there should be some reference to them. I shall therefore say something about two of his suggestions that seem to me doubtful. His main contention about the relevance of logic to philosophy does not depend, of course, on the correctness of each of his analyses.

I wish, then, to consider first his remarks about Hume and necessary connexion. In the third section of his paper he argues that a particular event E is explained when a statement e recording it is shown to be derivable from two independently established premisses, namely, from u, a universal statement or law, and i, a statement about certain initial conditions I. He thinks that the necessity by which E is said to be connected with I is really the necessity of the conjunction of E with I in relation to the law u, and that Hume's mistake consisted in neglecting u. I agree that Hume did not say enough about the explicit formulation of laws, and that he talked psychology of a rather dubious kind when he should have talked logic. But I do not think that Dr. Popper's account of the matter does justice to our ordinary usage of the phrase " necessary connexion ". When we say that E is necessarily connected with I, we do not mean merely that e follows logically from i and some universal statement u. We wish also to convey that u states a necessary connexion between kinds of events, and the fundamental problem is to explain the usage of " necessary connexion " in this latter context.

Many philosophers hold that a law of nature can be no more than a universal material implication, *i.e.*, something which could be expressed in a sentence of the form " For all

χ, it is not the case that χ is ϕ and χ is not ψ ". But this seems unsatisfactory ; for we suppose that we can derive contrary-to-fact conditionals from laws of nature, and we certainly cannot derive them from universal material implications. From the premiss that all the men in the next room are playing poker we cannot conclude that if the Archbishop of Canterbury *were* in the next room (which he is not) he *would be* playing poker. We can infer only that if the Archbishop *is* in the next room he *is* playing poker—a proposition which has no interest for us when we already know that he is not in the next room. It may perhaps be said in reply that laws of nature differ from propositions about all the men in the next room as not involving any restriction to a finite region of space or a finite period of time. No doubt this is true, but it makes a difference to the argument. For if the logical form of a law of nature is supposed to be otherwise the same as that of a proposition about all the men in the next room, its consequences must be supposed to be same *mutatis mutandis*. Our statements of natural law purport, then, to be something more than universal material implications, and I suggest we should say boldly that they are statements of necessary connexions which we cannot hope to know *a priori*. I know that it is very unfashionable to speak of necessary connexions in this way, but I can see no other way of doing justice to the ordinary thought of plain men and scientists.

Secondly, I wish to say something about Dr. Popper's remarks on freedom and responsibility. In the fourth section of his paper, which is concerned mainly with determinism, he says that we do not consider human behaviour either praiseworthy or blameworthy when it can be explained in the sense already mentioned without the help of *ad hoc* hypotheses, *i.e.*, when it can be brought under generalizations about the behaviour of all (or most) men in certain circumstances. And from this he concludes that conduct is morally free in so far as it is not causally explicable on independently ascertainable initial conditions. I agree that we do not praise or blame men for behaviour which can be brought under generalizations about what all (or most) men do in certain circumstances. If a man gives away the names of his friends under excruciating tortue, we say that he cannot be held responsible. But it seems strange to say that a man's conduct is free only when it is unpredictable. I may be sure that a friend will behave rightly in certain circumstances and yet think that his conduct will be free and deserving of praise. Does Dr. Popper want to deny this ? If not, how are we to interpret his remark about freedom and causality ? Does he mean that prediction based on knowledge of a man's character is fundamentally different from causal prediction ?

(4)

In all that I have said so far I have deliberately avoided making any generalizations about philosophical problems, partly because their nature is the subject of another symposium, but partly also because I doubt whether it is possible to provide a simple formula which will cover them all. I certainly do not wish to maintain that they are all problems of logic in a narrow sense of that word, or even that we shall cease to be perplexed about them when we are as well versed in logic as we should be. On the contrary, it seems to me that some of the most interest-problems, *e.g.*, that of the relation of mind and body, have little, if anything, to do with logic. I admit, of course, that we know fairly well what problems are to be called philosophical ; and I suppose that these must have some features in common, since a man who is interested in one of the group is usually interested also in the others. If I am pressed to say what this common element is, then I am inclined to agree with the view that they all have to do with the ways in which we use words. But I think this way of characterizing philosophical problems should be subject to two reservations.

In the first place, philosophical problems do not arise in the void. They arise during our use of language for nonphilosophical purposes, and they can rarely, if ever, be solved without some study of subjects other than logic and linguistics. Dr. Popper has drawn attention to the fact that they often contain an empirical element, and it would be easy to pile up examples in illustration of this. I shall refer only to the problem of the relation of body and mind which I have already mentioned. Anyone who thinks he can solve, or dissolve, this problem without paying any attention to the findings of neurologists or the inquiries of psychical researchers, must be very simple-minded or very doctrinaire. I do not say that neurology itself will provide an answer, not yet that we should accept any of the claims made by psychical researchers, but that the problem arises in such connexions as these and cannot be considered profitably without reference to them. If we professed to solve it from the logic book and the dictionary alone, we should make ourselves as ridiculous as any dogmatic metaphysicians of the past. It seems to me conceivable that the problem may be philosophical and yet insoluble in practice until empirical science has made much more progress. This does not mean that a philosophical solution would be of the same kind as a scientific hypothesis, but that our difficulty in getting the issue clear may be due to some limitation of our non-philosophical knowledge. The history of philosophical thinking about space provides an illustration of what I have in mind.

Secondly, when we say that philosophical problems have to do with the ways in which we use words, we do not prescribe a method for solving any single philosophical problem. For each problem must be solved in its own way. That is what we mean by calling it a problem. And so, if we accept this view of philosophy, we are not committed to any set of philosophical views. In particular we are not committed to saying that philosophical problems are pseudo-questions which disappear when we adopt a certain manner of speaking. For this latter thesis is not merely a general characterization of philosophy, but a claim to have solved all the problems of philosophy, and it must stand or fall by the success or failure of its defenders in dealing with all the particular problems commonly called philosophical. In my opinion it falls.

III.—*By* A. J. AYER.

I AGREE with Dr. Popper that there are philosophical problems. But merely to say this does not carry us very far. We want to know what it is about a problem that makes it philosophical ; how, for example, the method of philosophy differs from the method of a natural science ; and to this question neither Dr. Popper nor Mr. Kneale gives at all a clear answer. Dr. Popper speaks favourably of logical analysis, but he does not say what he takes logical analysis to be ; and while he implies that there are some philosophical problems that are not soluble, or not wholly soluble, by logical analysis, he does not say what these problems are or what other methods are required to solve them. Mr. Kneale makes the point that formal logic is itself a subject for philosophers to study, but neither he nor Dr. Popper makes any serious attempt to show how the study of formal logic will help philosophers to answer questions in other fields. Again, they both allow that philosophical problems may contain an empirical element, but they do not give any account of the way in which empirical questions enter into philosophy, nor do they show how the philosopher's treatment of them differs, say, from that of the natural scientist. Dr. Popper does indeed make one promising suggestion : that philosophical problems have what he calls " a second-storey character ", but he does not develop it. No doubt these problems are, as he says, " connected with questions *about* science, or *about* mathematics, or *about* art ", but as he does not go on to say how they are so connected, his statement does not tell us very much. Neither is it very helpful to be told that " philosophical answers must always remain tentative ". Dr. Popper makes this remark as the " proper reply " to the question how philosophical statements are tested ; but so far from its being the proper reply to this question, it is not a reply to it at all. If the answers must remain tentative, then presumably the tests, whatever they may be, are inconclusive ; but to say that the tests are inconclusive is not to tell us what they are. And why is Dr. Popper so sure that there cannot be a " definite, established answer " to any philosophical problem ? If, as I think he holds, no scientific theory should ever be regarded as finally established, it is because it may at any time be falsified by further observation. But then he tells us that the situation in philosophy is worse because of " the absence of empirical tests." Why is it worse ? I suppose because a philosophical theory cannot in that case be confirmed by any observation. But if it cannot be confirmed then neither can it in this way be refuted. And if philosophical theories are not subject to empirical tests, what sort of theories are they ? One possible answer would be that they were logical ; but this Dr. Popper hesitates to give. Nor would it square with his view that philosophical answers must always remain tentative. For I suppose he would allow that on logical issues a more positive decision was theoretically attainable.

At this point I think that Dr. Popper might reply that we all know well enough what a philosophical problem is, at least in the sense that we are able to recognize one when we come across it, and that it is a mistake to try to give a general definition of philosophy, or to specify the character of philosophical method. I think he might say that to attempt anything of this sort would be to take up the " aprioristic " attitude with which he reproaches the postivists. But what is wrong with this aprioristic attitude ? In so far as philosophical questions are not empirical, what other attitude towards them is possible ? Dr. Popper is very hard upon the positivists, but not, so far as I can see, with any very good reason. Thus, he repeats the old objection that any attempt to formulate their criterion of meaning must be self-defeating ; on the ground that a proposition to the effect that all significant propositions must either be empirical or else be, in some sense, propositions of logic, is itself neither empirical nor a proposition of logic. But I do not admit this. It seems to me that such a proposition can perfectly well be taken either as an empirical statement about what people mean by " meaning " ; or else, what seems to me preferable as a prescriptive definition ; and in that case it may be held to belong to logic. No doubt it then legislates for itself, but I do not see that this is necessarily vicious. Dr. Popper refers darkly to the paradox of the liar, but he does not show that in this case any paradox arises. And if he wishes to make it a rule that no proposition can significantly refer to itself, how does this differ from the type of aprioristic assertion to which he objects ?

Apart from an unsubstantiated charge of verbalism, the only other reason that Dr. Popper gives for condemning the positivists is that some of them have been addicted to phenomenalism. For he looks upon phenomenalism, and indeed upon sense-datum theories in general, as " aprioristic systems ". This is a change from the usual accusation that the introduction of sense-data is a piece of dubious psychology, and to my mind a change for the better. For, as I have argued elsewhere, those who maintain that we directly observe sense-data, as opposed to physical objects, are not putting forward an empirical hypothesis ; they are laying down a convention. They are proposing to describe certain features of our experience in a different way from that in which they are ordinarily described. And the point of doing this is that the fact, if it is a fact, that our ordinary perceptual statements can be interpreted as statements about sense data throws light upon their meaning. Similarly, the fact, if it is a fact, that it can be described in the terminology of sense-data tells us something about the character of our experience. Thus the sense-datum theory is aprioristic only in the sense in which any choice of concepts is aprioristic. And it does not follow from this, as Dr. Popper seems to think, that it is in any way dogmatic, or even that it is arbitrary.

I dwell upon this example of phenomenalism because the consideration of it may help us to see a little more clearly what it is that we are doing when we philosophize. I take it that the philosophical problem of perception is the problem of giving a logical analysis of perceptual statements. Now the phenomenalist's way of dealing with this problem is to invent an artificial language and to try to show that the perceptual statements, which it is his purpose to analyse, are translatable into it. Whether he is successful or not is a point that I am not now discussing. To this extent, his method is aprioristic, and his answer to the problem takes the form of a logical statement. His analysis results in saying that two sets of statements are logically equivalent ; or, if he does not go so far as this, it results in saying that certain statements of the one class are entailed by statements of the other. There is, however, an important sense in which his method is not aprioristic. For the language of sense-data is not constructed arbitrarily. It is intended to describe the facts by which our ordinary perceptual statements are verified. The position is not that we first invent the language of sense-data and then look round to see what it can be used for. Sense-data are brought in as a consequence of our reflecting upon what we mean by perceptual statements ; that is, as a consequence of our reflecting upon the nature of the facts which verify them. These facts are discovered to be complex in a way that is not very clearly brought out by our usual manner of describing them ; and the language of sense-data is brought in to do justice to this complexity. But what is this procedure of " reflecting upon the facts " ? I suggest that it takes the form of considering what are the situations that would make a given proposition true. Now since any answer to this question must consist in a description of these situations, what we get by these means is the replacement of one form of description by another. And so it may look as if we never leave the field of logic. Yet there is a sense in which we do leave it. It is not as if in order to discover the correct re-description we merely looked up an agreed table of linguistic rules. It is rather that we put ourselves imaginatively into some situation in which the statement we are analysing would be true, and try to make it out in detail. This process of making it out in detail is indeed a process of re-describing it ; but there is a sense, I think, in which our new description may give us a clearer insight into the facts. If you like, this is only another way of saying that it may enlighten us about the meaning of the statement we are analysing. But that it *is* another way of saying this seems to me important.

But how is the validity of such an analysis to be tested ? Principally, I think, by looking for counter-examples. We try to find a case in which one of the statements we are comparing would be true and the other false ; and if we do find such a case we conclude that they are not equivalent. Thus those who reject phenomenalism sometimes try to show that there is no proper equivalent in the sense-datum language for a statement to the effect that unobserved physical objects are causally related. They have maintained that the sensory statement which is supposed to be such an equivalent may be true in cases where the statement about the physical objects is false. I do not myself think that they are right in this contention ; but if they were they would have refuted the phenomenalists' analysis. The method is logical in the sense that finding a counter-example brings out a difference in the logical relations of the statements in question ; the conclusion reached is perhaps that some statement which is entailed by one of them is not entailed by the other, or possibly that some statements which are evidence for the one are not in the same degree evidence for the other. But these conclusions are not reached by *a priori* calculation. We do not come to them simply by applying a known set of transformation rules. It is rather that by means of them we may hope to discover what the transformation rules of our language are.

So long as we cannot find a counter-example, we may hold that our analysis is valid ; but I suppose it is always possible that some counter-example may be discovered. To that extent Dr. Popper is justified in his remark that " philosophical answers must always remain tentative ". But what if the answer in question is negative ? Even if we are never entitled to say of a philosophical theory that it is definitely established, are there not some philosophical theories of which we may say that they can be definitely refuted ? An instance which comes to my mind is the causal theory of perception. I think it can be shown that if the causal theory were true we should have no good reason to believe in the truth of any statement about a physical object ; and since it is a fact that we do have very good reason to believe in the truth of a great many statements about physical objects, it follows that the causal theory of perception is false. Put more formally, my argument is that statements about our sensory experiences which are evidence for the truth of ordinary perceptual statements are not in the same way evidence for the truth of the causal statements to which according to the causal theory, these perceptual statements are supposed to be equivalent. That is my counter-example. It may not be satisfactory ; many philosophers would deny that it was ; but if it is satisfactory, then it definitely refutes the causal theory. My point here is that if a philosophical theory is false, there is a way of disproving it ; and I see no reason why such disproof should not be allowed to be conclusive. What is not clear is that there is any way of definitely proving a philosophical theory to be true.

A better illustration of these points may perhaps be drawn from one of Dr. Popper's examples. Towards the close of his paper he puts it forward, as an empirical fact, that in so far as people believe that someone's behaviour can be "causally explained", they "do not think that it is either praiseworthy or blameworthy" ; and from this he apparently draws the conclusion that to say that a person has acted freely is equivalent to saying that we cannot assign any cause to his action. That is, it sometimes happens that our knowledge of the "initial conditions" which obtain in the given situation, together, presumably, with our knowledge of the laws which govern human behaviour in general, is not such that we can derive from it a satisfactory causal explanation of the action in question ; and to say that this is so is supposed to be equivalent to saying that the agent acted freely, and was therefore morally responsible for what he did. Now it seems to me, as it does to Mr. Kneale, that this conclusion is incorrect. And what convinces me that it is incorrect is that I can fairly easily conceive of counter-examples. Thus a lunatic may act unpredictably, but we do not for that reason conclude that he is morally responsible. And conversely, there are many cases in which we have no difficulty at all in accounting for the way that a person has behaved, and yet are still prepared to say that he was a free agent. The fact is, as I see it, that the actions for which people are praised or blamed are those in which some choice of the agent's is a causal factor. Thus the decisive question is not *whether* we can explain the action or not, but *how* we explain it. So long as the explanation is in terms of the agent's own character and choices we are inclined to say that he has acted freely. The cases in which we are inclined to say that he has not acted freely, and so is not morally responsible, are those in which the agent's choice is either not a causal factor at all, or else an insignificant factor. In such cases it is said that the agent could not help himself, either because it is thought that he would have acted in the same way no matter what he had decided, or else because the circumstances were such that no reasonable man would have chosen otherwise. Thus, if someone points a pistol at my head with the result that I surrender to his wish, there is a sense in which I could have disobeyed him ; but if what he demands of me is such that no reasonable man would sacrifice his life rather than grant it, then even though what I do is something that would have been considered wrong if I had done it deliberately, I am not held to blame for it. I am acquitted on the ground that I acted under duress. The mistake which Dr. Popper and many others have made is that of confusing causation with compulsion. No doubt in any case in which I act under duress my action is causally explicable ; but the converse does not hold. It is not true that whenever my action is causally explicable I act under duress.

This analysis of moral freedom would need a great deal more elaboration for it to do justice to the facts ; but at present I am more interested in the question of method. It is to be noted that Dr. Popper starts out with an empirical statement, and that from it he derives a logical rule. Mr. Kneale and I reject his logical rule, but our grounds for rejecting it seem to be empirical. We say that it does not correspond to the way in which people actually use the word "freedom"; that people are in fact held morally responsible for actions for which they would not be responsible if Popper's rule held good. So it looks as if we are all engaged in a sociological investigation. But if we are engaged in a sociological investigation, our manner of proceeding is most unscientific. For we do not seriously set about collecting evidence. We seem content rather to take our own usage as standard. We imagine various situations and consider how we would describe them. This gives us a list of examples from which we extract a logical rule; and then we test the rule by trying it on further examples. The argument is thus to a certain extent *ad hominem*. A philosopher makes what seems to be a logical statement; he says that such and such an expression is equivalent to such and such another. You then ask him how he would describe a certain situation, assuming that he will describe it in the same way as you do yourself. And then you point out to him that, as he uses them in this instance, the two expressions are not equivalent. There is also the underlying assumption that the usage upon which you both agree is a standard usage. But this seems always to be taken for granted in philosophical discussions. It is a point that is never seriously investigated.

There is, however, another way of looking at the matter. In the case of free will, for example, a philosopher may come to think that the distinction which we draw between actions for which the agent is held responsible, and those for which he is not held responsible is unduly artificial. Why should we attach so much importance to the fact that the agent's choice is in some cases itself a causal factor, seeing that it may be possible to give a causal explanation of his choice in terms of some previous set of initial conditions, and that this process may eventually carry us beyond the series of his choices altogether? Now the critic who argues in this way wishes to emphasize the resemblance between the cases in which people are held accountable for their actions and those in which they are not. He does not deny that there is a difference between the two types of cases, but he wishes to suggest that this difference is unimportant. It does not seem to him a sufficient ground for making moral judgments. Accordingly, he shifts the ground. He may, like Dr. Popper, make what seems to be the false empirical statement that we praise or blame people only in the cases where we are unable to explain why they act as they do. But this is not to be taken as a straightforward empirical statement. It is an encouragement to us to give up making moral judgments of this sort. The suggestion is that we should not be inclined to make them if we knew more of the facts ; and that therefore it is unreasonable for us to make them as it is. In short, the analysis is not descriptive but persuasive. I do not say that this is what Dr. Popper himself is doing, though it is a plausible interpretation of what he says. If it is his procedure, then I may point out that he too is an " apriorist ", though not, so far as this goes, in any vicious sense.

Much the same questions arise in regard to the example which occupies the main part of Dr. Popper's paper, his analysis of causation. As he himself admits, this analysis is very sketchy ; but if he claims no more than that there are *some* cases in which it is correct to say of two events which are related in the manner he describes that one of them is the cause of the other, I think that he is right. The conditions that he mentions are not sufficient even in these cases ; but I dare say that he would not find it difficult to make the necessary amplifications. I think also that he has given a correct account of what is very often meant by " explanation ". On the other hand I do not think that he is right in his view that explanation always takes the form that he describes. It seems to me that in history, and indeed in the field of human action generally, giving an explanation is very often not a matter of appealing to universal laws but rather a matter of telling more of the story. We are satisfied when the story takes on a familiar pattern ; and here Dr. Popper might reply that the reason why we are so satisfied is that it then comes to exemplify some universal law. But I do not think that this is true.

It is sufficient for us if the account that we are given describes one of the ways in which we should expect such things to happen, and we do not need to believe that they always happen so. I do not say that in such cases no universal laws are discoverable, but only that the knowledge of them is not essential to the process of explanation. Accordingly, if Dr. Popper means to describe our actual usage, I think that he is wrong to take the sort of explanation that occurs in physics as his only model. But here again it is not clear to me whether he means to describe how we do use a term or to prescribe how we should.

I disagree also with what he says about necessity. He claims that his analysis of causation enables him to solve "Hume's problem", but he seems to have an inaccurate conception of what Hume's problem was. To begin with it is a travesty of Hume's position to say that he made "an attempt at causally explaining away causality". What Hume was concerned to show was first, that from a proposition describing the occurrence of a particular event, considered by itself, it was not possible to deduce anything about the occurrence of any other event; secondly, that general propositions which affirmed the connection of two distinct events were not logically necessary; and thirdly, that such terms as "power" and "force", as applied to the relations between particular events, did not stand for anything observable. And with all these propositions I assume that Dr. Popper would agree. He would in any case be wrong if he did not. At the same time Hume thought that he had an idea of "necessary connexion", and since he believed that every idea must correspond to a previous impression, he set about looking for an impression from which this idea could be derived. He found it, as we all know, in the propensity of our minds to associate the ideas of objects which had frequently been experienced in conjunction. Now I do not think that Hume's account of the way in which we come by our alleged idea of "necessary connexion" is very convincing. The question is psychological; and I believe that a psychological investigation would show that the idea that people had of causal necessity was very confused, and that it was partly derived from primitive experiences of pushing and pulling, and partly perhaps a relic of animism. But I do not press these suggestions. What I wish to point out is that Dr. Popper does not go into this question at all. For all the harsh things that he says about " apriorism ", his method here is thoroughly aprioristic. What he does is to lay down a usage for the term " necessary connexion ". He proposes that we shall say that E is necessarily connected with I when there is some well established law u, from which, in conjunction with the proposition i affirming the existence of I, a proposition e, affirming the existence of E, is formally deducible.

Now for my part I do not much care for this proposal. It seems to me to have the great demerit of reviving the confusion between logical and causal necessity which it was Hume's great achievement to have exposed. For the point is that e is not entailed by i. It is entailed by it only in conjunction with u. And u itself is not necessary. Dr. Popper says " we need not believe in the necessity, or even in the truth, of u to see that given u, e can be logically obtained from i " ; and this is true. But if all that were required for E and I to be necessarily connected were that there was some premiss which in conjunction with i entailed e, then every event would be necessarily connected with every other. For it is always possible to find some proposition which will fulfil this purely formal condition. If there is to be a causal connection between I and E it is necessary not only that ui should entail e but that u should be true. If Dr. Popper is right, it is also requisite that we should have good reason to believe that u is true. Thus, as he himself recognizes, to assert that E and I are necessarily connected will be a way of expressing the strength of our belief in u. But we already express this by saying that E and I are causally connected. What do we gain then, on Dr. Popper's scheme, by saying that this connexion is necessary? In my opinion, only confusion can result from it.

On much the same grounds I object also to Mr. Kneale's proposal that we should regard u itself as the expression of a necessary connexion. I am inclined to agree with him that the relation of material implication does not reflect our normal use of " if . . . then " as it occurs in variable hypotheticals. I find this use of " if . . . then " very difficult to analyse, and I can see that Mr. Kneale might wish to introduce some technical term to mark its peculiarity. But for obvious historical reasons, I do not think that " necessary connexion " is at all suitable for the purpose.

I have concentrated mainly on Dr. Popper's paper, and have not left myself time to deal with the many interesting points that are raised by Mr. Kneale's. But I should like just to refer to his proof that there are synthetic *a priori* propositions. As he defines his terms, the proof is valid; but for my taste his definition of " analytic " is too narrow. I should prefer to keep the term " analytic " for propositions " whose truth is guaranteed by the rules of usage of the symbols they contain ", and use some other term, perhaps " tautological " to refer to the sub-class of analytic propositions which consists of those that are demonstrable within a given system. But I recognize that this notion of " being guaranteed by a rule of usage " needs rather more explanation than it has hitherto received.

THINGS AND PERSONS.

Prof. D. M. MacKinnon, Prof. H. A. Hodges and Mr. John Wisdom.

I.—*By* D. M. MacKinnon.

It is a commonplace today to say that metaphysics is impossible. Indeed, the demonstration of the impossibility of metaphysics has assumed the status less of an exercise for philosophers than a stock in trade essay for students. Yet one may question whether some of those who with such assurance rule the claims of the metaphysical philosopher out of court have altogether taken the measure of what he is about.

Now the subject of this paper is a metaphysical theory—that is to say what we shall be concerned with is something which Collingwood might have called a set of presuppositions, but whose character can perhaps be described without the use of that question-begging term. Of course, metaphysical theories differ enormously in character, but at least it seems that they resemble one another in this, that they prescribe absolutely the kind of discussions their champions think worth undertaking, and at the same time dictate the moves they make in the course of their argumentation. Thus, even if one agrees with those who say that philosophy can be more or less reduced to logic or the study of the inter-relation of the various current systems of common sense and scientific description, one has to allow the presence in the background for this conception, of unsuspected presuppositions concerning what is worth saying as well as what is sayable. It is hard to see how one can offer a purely logical criterion of what is sayable, even though one may concede the character of logical to those operations whereby one determines the formation and transformation rules of some individual system of representation. The problem of what can be said, the analysis of " can " in that phrase remains one of the cruces of contemporary philosophy. And we are perhaps not much further on than Kant was, at least in the elaboration of a method for solving it.

None the less it remains true that those philosophers who have gone furthest in the direction I have indicated would repudiate altogether the suggestion that their concern to restrict philosophical inquiry in this way was governed by anything other than a recognition of its proper scope. The suggestion that all utterance, which does not thus fall within the scope of the "language of science" or those languages whose logical relation to the "language of science" can be plotted, should be dismissed as trivial or meaningless is commended as a surgical operation demanded by the nature of things. It is, perhaps, unfortunate that one cannot resist the sense that this conception of the nature of things, however subtle its characterisation, does retain something of the character of a metaphysical theory. And that in effect however much the playing of the game may essay stand pointlessness that stand pointlessness is by no means completely achieved.

Now in this paper I want to revert to a very crude and primitive essay in what may be called the elimination of the metaphysical, so crude that the metaphysical characters of the presupposition of the operation itself are hardly concealed. I am referring to an aspect of the work of the so-called utilitarians. I take this example deliberately because the subject matter of this symposium is presumably primarily ethical, and it seems to me that the utilitarian attitude towards ethical problems illustrates excellently, in the field of ethics, the extent to which the attack on metaphysics is itself governed by a kind of metaphysical bias. Utilitarianism remains enormously interesting not simply for what it is as an ethical theory, but because it represents an explicit attitude towards the problem of conduct that reveals how that problem must appear to anyone who tries resolutely to eliminate from the discussion any appeal whatsoever to that which transcends observation.

In a textbook on ethics you will find utilitarianism usually listed as the theory which insists that the rightness or wrongness of actions be judged by a reference to their consequences. But if you read widely the history of the subject you find that the contours of the doctrine cease easily to be contained by this description. For utilitarianism as professed by the most important of those who argue and develop the theory was much more than a series of propositions. It could much more accurately be described as the programme of a campaign, whether on the plane of philosophical analysis or at the level of social reform. Of course the whole argument pivoted on the ancient question of the relation of the "ought" to the "is". True the logical apparatus at the disposal of the utilitarians was as defective as their psychological theories of the spring of conduct. But their purpose was fundamentally clear; and likewise their assumption. They insisted that ethics must be regarded as nearly as possible as a system of fact, albeit a system of fact of a very special sort. When Godwin in his "Political Justice" described morality as a system of public advantage, he wrote as a utilitarian. Although the psychology the utilitarians employed was crudely introspective in technique, there underlay their attitude to human needs and wants the conviction that these were in no way typically different from any other fact in the world.

Of course to understand them, to understand the game they were playing one must understand also what suggested to them that this was the way to play the game, and moreover one must understand the game their opponents were playing. In other words, of course, one must study them historically, in the circumstances of their origin. And it is, I would insist, a gross mistake to suppose that such a method is incompatible with concern for the truth or falsity of their doctrine. Rather it alone helps one to see what actually that doctrine was, and in seeing to judge something of what philosophy always comes near being to the empiricist. Thus if one points to the extent to which the utilitarians found their inspiration in Newtonian physics, one is neither ignoring the importance of e.g. Bentham's concern with legal reform nor the permanent significance of the utilitarian outlook. One is neither confining the inspiration of the utilitarian to the methods of the exact sciences, nor is one suggesting that the utilitarian attitude belongs in a peculiar measure to a particular moment in the development of scientific method and understanding. Fundamentally, the utilitarian champions the ideal of an ethics not mysterious, of principles of human behaviour most related to, because derived from, the scrutiny of the facts of that behaviour and from the latent possibilities of adjustment and harmonisation to which it is judged to be open. Neither in that behaviour nor in the principles by which it is to be judged is there anything mysterious. Observation will reveal its nature and observation too will suggest the kind of modification to which its initial springs are susceptible.

Here one should emphasise two points as of fundamental importance :—

1. In the language of the late Professor John Laird, utilitarianism is an act-ethic—that is, an ethic concerned to study primarily the properties of acts. As nearly as possible the utilitarian, for all the fact that his psychological method is crudely introspective, thinks of an act as a transaction, as a change in a medium whose form is conceived as being as closely as possible analogous to a physical system : granted that such transactions are malleable, can be modified in their direction and consequence by legislative interference, it is still insisted that fundamentally the moralist finds his field in acts, a very special class of event, with the difference between them and physical events reduced to a minimum.

2. In utilitarianism you have a doctrine that from one point of view appears rigid : whereas from another it possesses a curious flexibility. It is rigid in its insistence that acts be judged by nothing apart from their result. Moral judgment need take no account of the deliverances of any intuition or moral sense : no traditional sanctities can defend themselves against criticism by appeal to a sixth sense. It is rigid too in its insistence on happiness as

something relatively simple, possessed of no interior complexity of structure. Yet it is flexible in its conviction that human nature is sufficiently malleable to permit our finding our satisfaction in vastly different kinds of objective.

You may ask why we should waste time on such familiar considerations. Simply for this reason. In utilitarianism one encounters a clear example, clear to the point of a caricature of the approach to ethics which refuses altogether to take personal existence seriously. You see this in the insistence that the notion of happiness is fundamentally simple, that in effect happiness can be so defined as to constitute the turn of the whole analysis. It is insisted that in human satisfaction there is nothing mysterious. As James Mill boasted, " given time, one should be able to make the human mind as clear as the road from Charing Cross to St. Paul's ". Now it is perfectly true that the contemporary empiricist has seen the logical contradiction in the notions of absolute simplicity and of absolute clarity. As Ramsey said " One can make nothing clear but one can hope to make many things clearer ". But for all that it remains true that in that process of clarification the contemporary successors of the utilitarians will insist that the idea of satisfaction can be invoked to clarify, rather than referred to as something requiring clarification.

In this criticism of the utilitarian doctrine in the form which we encounter it in Shaftesbury, Butler attacked it on the ground that you could not derive from the utilitarian doctrine a satisfactory conception of the virtuous life. Yet in effect a utilitarian might reply that this was simply to miss the mark inasmuch as it implied that it was the virtuous life which mattered and not the system of public advantage. To say, as Butler does, that benevolence is not the whole of virtue is to insist that the life of the morally good man is not necessarily achieved simply by disinterested concern for the good of others. The relations in which a man stands to his fellows are not exhausted in terms of benefactor confronting beneficiary and so on. There are other kinds of situations which morally engage a man for instance, there is the promise made or the demand of justice. Butler protests against the utilitarian refusal to discriminate satisfactions, against his readiness to treat goods as homogeneous. But he does this because he has in effect departed from the whole method characteristic of the utilitarian, and indeed of act-ethics in general. He argues that the proper subject of the moralist is the individual or person in his nature and in his relations with his fellows, and he refuses consequently to allow that we can so to speak absorb ethical reflection in discussion of the means of promoting good or find the primary field for the application of our ethical idea in (to quote Godwin's phrase again) a system of public advantage.

All this I mention because it seems that the work of such thinkers as Kierkegaard, Buber, Marcel and the rest is best approached if it is seen in relation to an opposition with which every student of ethics is familiar—that is to say, the opposition between the assessment of ethical principle as significant primarily in relation to the promotion of a system of public advantage, and that which insists that the primary sense of such ideas be found in the personal existence of the individual, in his relations to his fellows. I have said nothing of Kant who perhaps more obviously than Butler in his doctrine of the good will repudiates at once the idea of goods as in any sense homogeneous and the possibility of treating moral relations and principles out of relation to choice and its determination. But clearly his position is one that insists on acts as significant to the moralist qua " pieces of living " and not as transactions.

To set the writers I have just mentioned in the tradition outline may seem strange : especially in view of the fact that Kierkegaard from whom both Buber and Marcel in varying ways derived is best known as a critic as Hegel, and Hegel surely must be thought of as standing not so much in the following of the utilitarian as that of their opponents. It was, however, primarily against the impersonal element in Hegel, his doctrine of the sovereignty of the universal idea, that Kierkegaard sought to defend the significance and ultimacy of personal existence ; and for us the significance of what he was about is perhaps equally clearly seen if one reflects on what ethics must rot away into if the assumption of the homogeneity of satisfaction is accepted, and ethical principles construed primarily as the means of constructing a system of public advantage.

I suppose that the student of traditional ethics coming first to such writers as I have mentioned is impressed by the sense that in them the frontiers between philosophical analysis and literary description seem to have been passed. Would you describe Kierkegaard as philosopher, theologian, psychologist, writer of dramatic dialogue? His aversion to generalisation goes much further than hostility to "the system". The enunciation of general theses of any kind seem to dissolve away into a prolonged series of descriptions. His comparison of lives and attitudes of mind, even though in places it recalls Plato, is concrete: Socrates, Abraham, Job, Don Juan, and—he will never withdraw from the particular into the characterisation of some form of life as good as such. One is far withdrawn from Kant, for instance, in Kant's insistence that the form of the good life can be characterised apart from the matter; there is nothing remotely resembling the sort of formal logic of moral conduct you get in the Grundlegung. At times one cannot resist the impression that principle is altogether abandoned in the interest of an inwardness realised perhaps as much by the rogue as by the saint. One cannot talk easily in brief about Kierkegaard: one can only commend him, as perhaps he would have wished to be commended, as a corrective. For in the last resort, as he insists, his work can only be understood in relation to himself: it is the record of his own pilgrimage that he has left. One cannot detach principles or criticise their absence: fundamentally, his most important communications are always in his own phrase indirect. Yet perhaps it is only to be expected that it is just this fact that his ideas are so hard to catch hold of that makes the professional philosopher so impatient with him. None the less he must be reckoned with; for no one has seen more clearly than he that the category of individuality is that on which any generalised speculation must suffer shipwreck. What it is to be an individual is not something whose contents can be expounded : it can only, he argues, be shown and that indirectly.

So too in other ways with the other thinkers I have mentioned, both alike are on edge in the presence of the general or the abstract, and argue, if I understand them aright, that the sense of such fundamental ideas of personal existence as meeting, encounter, hope, loyalty, is lost if we seek to offer of them a general definition irrespective of the circumstances of the individual. The only definition one can possibly offer is by way of example. For it is of the very nature of such relations that they engage men as individuals, exposing them not as instances of such and such abstract characters but as this or that man. Whereas certainly such an ethic as Butler's or Kant's is fundamentally right against the utilitarian in insisting that ethical ideas find definition in the field of personal existence, they are wrong if they suppose that such can be conceived in terms of a general formula. The use of any such formula can only have the effect of drawing an artificial boundary to contain that which in its nature cannot be contained. The responsiveness of men to men, the " disponability " of a man in the presence of his fellows, the diversity of human love—these are not things that can be mapped. You cannot set out even in the most rarified formula what is that which through the intimacies of personal exchange a man is called to become. Although certainly in human life it is the discipline of the ego that is at issue, you cannot simply define that discipline in terms of the submission of inclination to principle : to do that is to run the risk of conceiving the fundamental business of becoming human impersonally, in terms less of a man's relations with his fellows than of submission to the impersonal discipline of reason. If one identifies goodness with the taking of an objective view of one's behaviour, one is in danger of conceiving goodness out of relation to the actual situation in which it is realised : one runs the risk of that unconscious solipsism, of that withdrawal of oneself in idea from one's actual relations with one's fellows which for men like Buber and Marcel constitutes the fundamental state in ethics.

Whereas in Kierkegaard the idea of the individual takes shape in the exposition of an extraordinary complex and ultimately religious dialectic (in a dialectic that is almost Hegelian in its sinuosity and is throughout unified by the " leap " of faith), men like Buber and Marcel although the temper of their thought is religious, are much more concerned with ethical realities. That is to say, one can trace in what they are discussing a more evident kinship with the discussions of traditional moral philosophy. The situations they consider include familiar ones like the giving and receiving of promises ; only they urge us to ponder the inwardness of such situations and to see them in relation to the men and women who, they urge, come into being through them. One might say that whereas for the Kantian moral worth is constituted through the individual's submission to the discipline of practical reason, for writers of this school such worth is realised by the extent to which the individual so to speak opens and deepens himself through his relations to his fellows. But there is a kinship with the older intuitionism in the insistence on the hard inescapable facts of personal existence. Or so certainly it seems in some writers of this school who speak as if they sought to substitute for elementary consciousness of the Cartesian sort at the outsef of reflective construction, a man's sense of himself as standing over against his fellows, who make demands on him. And this for all the extraordinary subtlety, the attention to individual detail and the rest ; their thinking is less self-absorbed than Kierkegaard's, less sheerly religious in its movement, and, as I say at the outset, appeal is made to that which has something of the character of an a priori intuition.

Thus it is insisted both that the facts of personal moral exchange are unanalysable, and that they are evident to anyone who reflects on what he knows. Linguistic usage attests them, and here of course the well-known distinction between the language of " I " and " Thou ", the language of address, and the language of " It " that of description, is invoked. Certainly it is more and more recognised that where ethics is concerned, the language of conversation, of advocacy, of intreaty even is more important than that of description : it would be admitted that if we are to approach ethical study linguistically, it is to the function of such language that we must attend and its logic or principles that we must try to plot. But clearly writers of the kind I have mentioned go much further than that, and insist not simply that in ethics we concern ourselves with what such language expresses, but that we rate as of prior ontological significance the kind of reality to which it calls attention and it is argued that we only have to think in order to see that this is so. Maybe the appeal is not simply to intuition : but it is implied that the kind of reflection necessary to establish the authority of this kind of experience is comparatively short, even though of course, the content of the experience is practically inexhaustible. *One might perhaps say that with Buber we have seen a transformation of the older intuitive ethics into a thesis concerning the prior ontological significance of particular forms of speech* ; and again one returns, of course, to the question of the authority of such an intuition. With Kierkegaard it is different : his descriptions either do or do not establish themselves ; and their elaboration and subtlety give them every chance to do or not to do so.

But to recapitulate : writers like those I have mentioned are significant because in various ways they raise the problem of the individual. In a way they recall one strand in Kant, even though he would have regarded their thinking as lawless, and they are on edge in the presence of the rigidity with which he insists that we can plot the form of the good life. Yet they are one with him in insisting that the ethical problem is not one which can be reduced to a study of the mechanics of adjusting satisfactions. That is, they take the ethical problem seriously and insist that it is a problem. Or perhaps I make a mistake in using that general singular : it is problems that they take seriously, the problematic elements in human existence. Only of course in doing this, there is nothing self-authenticated.

If with Mill we say that it is better to be Socrates dissatisfied than a fool satisfied, we have still to recognise that this thesis does not simply authenticate itself. If one rates personal existence seriously, if one judges the work we have been concerned with as significant, one has still to justify that judgment. One still has, for instance, to vindicate the significance one claims for Kierkegaard's religious dialectic, and that problem, which is part of the problem of the possibility of metaphysics, is of course ultimately the problem of distinguishing things and persons. It seems to me that traditional ethics of what used to be called a non-naturalist pattern has always taken this distinction more or less for granted ; it has of course usually found the differentia of the person in the presence of reason, both practical and theoretical and in consequence, perhaps, it has failed adequately to schematise what personal existence is. It is to this problem that some contemporary writers, such as Buber and Marcel, have turned their attention ; while others, engaging with a more profound problem, have called attention to the extraordinary difficulty with which one retains hold of a sense of the person as significant against the manifold arguments in favour of treating it as somehow reducible to something other than itself. The problems which confront the moralist today in this connection are two-fold. There is the problem of what exactly it is to be a person ; and there is the further problem of how one authenticates the claim that one is inclined to make for characteristically personal existence. There is, of course, the further question of what precisely becomes of ethics as traditionally pursued outside the utilitarian school if one refuses to give any significance at all to the idea of person as distinct from thing. It is perhaps the status of our sense of the unconditional worth of the personal that lies back behind our controversies concerning ethical intuition.

II.—*By* H. A. Hodges.

Martin Buber and the philosophers who are known as "existentialists" are at one, despite all differences, in believing that what may be called "personal existence" is of the greatest practical concern to mankind. From this starting-point it is possible to move out in various directions. One might proceed to religious questions, or to that kind of metaphysical speculation whose motive is religious rather than logical. Professor Mackinnon has chosen to keep the discussion on the more accessible plane of traditional moral theory, and his contention is that the personalist writers have a contribution to make to moral theory which ought not to be neglected. I agree with him, and shall have little to say but to restate what I think is his fundamental contention from my own point of view.

Professor Mackinnon begins his paper with a discussion of utilitarianism and an exposure of its weakness. I should like to begin with a recognition of its merits; for it may be held that, by contrast with the intuitionist approach to moral theory which is current in some quarters, utilitarianism has at least its heart in the right place, though its head is muddled.

The charge against intuitionism is that, though it begins in a perfectly legitimate way, it stops short before coming to the heart of the subject. No doubt it is largely a matter of personal choice whether moral philosophy should begin by considering our sense of duty or by examining the idea of the good. No doubt real discoveries have been made in both ways. In particular, the exercise of analysing our sense of duty may sharpen our use of terms and our awareness of moral issues in a way that is both informative and beneficial. It may also lead to over-subtlety, and when we pass from the formulation and codification of commonly agreed moral judgments to the consideration of fictitious cases, as the enquiry usually leads us to do, it is easy to feel that the character of our thinking changes, and what began as an empirical enquiry into what the moral consciousness asserts is transformed into a profitless exercise of fancy. All that the intuitionist ethic can usefully do is to report what the moral consciousness of most people, in that society to which the philosopher writing it belongs, has to say on those questions on which it has reached a judgment at all. It can tell us what the moral judgment of our contemporaries says we ought to do. But, if we ourselves have reached a certain level of critical awareness, it cannot thereby convince us that we ought to do it. For, even if we share the moral consciousness of our contemporaries, and our own intuitive judgments are the same as theirs, yet by the very fact of being philosophers we are surely committed to calling these intuitions in question.

We are used to being told that the question " Why should I do my duty ? " is one which no one who understands the terms can ask. It needs little courage to call this bluff. No doubt if X is what I ought to do, I ought to do X. The question, however, is whether anything is really meant by saying that I " ought " to do anything, and whether this idea of " ought " really signifies anything for which a reasonably-ordered life could find a place. The classic tradition of moral philosophy has always held that the idea of " ought " is not primary and irreducible, and that judgments containing it can be derived from more ultimate judgments concerning what is " good " ; while it has also commonly been held that these in turn can be reduced to propositions about the nature of man and the world, together with expressions of, or propositions about, human desires and purposes. What I ought to do, in short, depends on what it would be best that I should do, and that in turn depends on what I am and what other things and people are, and what we all most constantly desire. To me it seems that, if duty does not in fact rest on this foundation, it hangs in the air ; in that case I do not know what it means and I do not recognise its claim over me.

Now, on this point utilitarianism is clear-sighted. Its *Leitmotif* is that laid down by Bentham in his attack on natural law, that there is nothing in *a priori* principles which cannot be better stated as an induction from experience, and that there is no means of distinguishing true principles from irrational prejudices except by applying this test. Utilitarianism also makes the point that principles, whether *a priori* or empirically grounded, are general and abstract, and that the concrete reality to which they refer and for whose sake they are formulated is the lives of human beings, their satisfactions and their frustrations. That is why the utilitarian philosophy did, in actual history, become the theoretical basis of a great reforming movement whose impetus is not yet spent. Wherever it is taken for granted that the object of law and government is the public good, and wherever moral codes and taboos are criticised from the standpoint of their effect in liberating or frustrating the energies of men, the utilitarian principle is at work. It is the principle that people matter, and that moral principles as well as public institutions are there only to serve the people.

If we are clear about this great merit of utilitarianism, we can go on to recognise its manifold faults in detail. These, or the worst of them, can be summed up in the Diltheian complaint that utilitarianism is not true to its own purposes. As Dilthey brings against 19th-century empiricism the charge that it is not empirical enough (*Empirie und nicht Empirismus* is his slogan), so he brings against utilitarianism the charge that it is not really concrete, that it merely substitutes one sort of abstractions for another. He claims to " trump utilitarianism ", to " show that it is a construction from above downwards ", and to " defend the concrete realities of the moral impulses against abstract principles ". Yet it was not his contention that there are no principles, or that moral judgments cannot be analysed and reduced to their ultimate elements. In moral theory, he says, as in aesthetics and educational theory, there are " all-pervading universally-valid rules ". They express the impact of social forces upon the conduct of the individual. No one can get on in the social system if he does not fit in to the various very subtle but unavoidable relationships which that system involves. There are laws which state that certain kinds of conduct tend to bring certain kinds of results ; and on these are based imperatives which tell people how, in the interests of society and in their own, they had better behave. The point is that the utilitarians enormously oversimplified the situation, and their version of the principles at work was superficial and unreal.

There are passages in Professor Mackinnon's paper where he seems to say that the reality of moral life cannot be expressed in general terms at all, and that no principles can be laid down for our guidance in this sphere. If this were really so, it would seem to mean that there is no such thing as moral philosophy, but only an art of intuitive perception in moral issues. This would agree well enough with the literary form of Kierkegaard's work and that of other existentialists, but it would confirm the suspicion with which the professional philosopher is apt to regard them. I do not see how a philosphical conference can embrace Professor Mackinnon's views unless their real meaning is something less than this, unless he really means to say, not that there are no principles, but that they are very various and very complex, and that any attempt to explain the moral life in terms of one or two principles of high generality, or to resolve a particular moral issue in that way, will fail to do justice to the demands of the concrete situation. If that is all he means, he joins the long succession of those who have protested against abstract moral theories in the name of life itself, and I go with him in the protest. I would even concede that the moral life is so complex that it is questionable whether any moral theory will be able to do justice to it ; the same is, I think, undoubtedly true of aesthetic experience. But the moral of this seems to be not that we should plunge ourselves into the psychological profundities of French or Danish philosophical journalism, but that we should heed Dilthey's call to moral philosophers to explore the diversity as well as the unity of the moral life.

To return to utilitarianism. In its hedonistic form it

was wrong as to the real object of human desire. That is a psychological error, and we may leave the psychologists to deal with it ; that is their business. But utilitarianism was wrong also in its conception of the relation between action and the end of action. For it worked throughout on the assumption that the end in view, the good which is sought, is something distinct from the action, whose result it is, and which is itself therefore a mere means to this end. It follows from this that the way to judge an action is not by any quality inherent in it, but by its consequences. Yet common experience shows, and Aristotle long ago pointed out, that we often perform actions for their own sake, the satisfaction lying in the action itself and not in its consequences. More, it is often the case that we find satisfaction neither in the outcome of an action nor in the inherent quality of the action itself, but in the place which it holds in a scheme of life and conduct, its relation to other actions in a whole which is felt to be good as a whole. The real value lies, as Mr. Joseph put it, in a " form of life ". The recognition of these facts takes us away beyond utilitarianism, but it takes us further along the same road, towards an honest consultation of experience.

The next stage will take us beyond Mr. Joseph's formula also, though not, I am sure, beyond his real meaning. For to speak of a " form of life " is to say something which might apply to the conduct of an individual taken in isolation. It implies a coherence in his actions, but this coherence might be contained within his personal existence, his own physical, psychological, and mental development, and his relations with other people and the physical world might be only means to this. But few of us will agree that this is in fact the moral good as conceived by ourselves or by the vast majority of our fellow-men. The relations with an external surrounding reality, which find expression in my actions, are themselves full of significance for me, and an important part of my happiness or unhappiness, a principal element in the quality of my life, lies in my consciousness of these relations. My interactions with the physical object in manual work, the regard I must pay to the properties of the materials I work with, and the sense of fruitful co-ordination when my efforts and the natural qualities of the object work together—the similar sense of purposeful collaboration or exhilarating opposition in my relations with physical objects in play—the sense of another life with which I have dealings in my relations with plants and still more with animals—and above all the recognition of a human being like myself, an *alter ego* who regards me as I regard him, and who impinges on me not only by automatic reactions but also and chiefly by conscious purposes and deliberate actions towards me—these relationships and the consciousness of them form a part of human life which is of central importance for our psychological health and our happiness. They are a happy hunting ground for the poets. A more rarefied kind of relationship, but not less real, is that between the human mind and that which confronts it, the object which the scientist explains or the artist contemplates, the living being or the human personality which the psychologist explains, the poet contemplates and portrays, or the historian understands and records. Philosophy makes a big mistake if it confines its interest in logic, in aesthetics, or in ethics to the processes which go on within the thinking, contemplating or deliberating mind, or the formal principles by which these processes are or should be guided, and overlooks the interplay between subject and object which is the very meaning of all these spheres of activity. But for ethics it is only the relationships with human beings which are of prime concern. In our intercourse with nature, important though it may be to us in many ways, we rarely seem to find moral questions coming up, whereas our relations with human beings seem to be the very province in which such questions are at home.

What is the fundamental relation which we desire to find between ourselves and other human beings, or between other human beings in our entourage? As Professor Mackinnon says, it is not merely beneficence. To think of the right relation between human beings as one in which each is the beneficiary of the rest is to fall far short of the truth. Indeed, it is common experience that when A does something for B, B values the action not primarily for itself, but for the evidence which he takes it to be of A's attitude towards him, and this attitude itself is what B chiefly prizes. Aristotle says in the *Poetics* that the plot of a play is more important than the characterisation, because it is in acting and being acted upon that we are happy or the reverse. However this may be in drama (and it is questionable whether modern drama is as true to this canon as the drama known to Aristotle was), it seems to be quite untrue in human relationships. What I chiefly want of my friend or neighbour is not to receive actual benefits from him, but to know that I have his good will, that he regards me with a friendliness which I can freely reciprocate. It is true that friendliness cannot exist without creating a disposition to serve one's friends. It is true also that we all depend in a great degree upon services rendered by one to another. Still I think it is true that we value such services even more for the good will to which they testify than for their inherent utility.

This good will is a kind of being-for-other. It is the "disponability" of which Professor Mackinnon speaks. What its expression in conduct may be will depend on the circumstances in which A and B are brought together, the nature and duration of the contacts between them. And I believe that mankind has always recognised certain broad distinctions between types of contact and relationship, assigning to each type the kind of behaviour which is considered to be the appropriate expression of good will in that relation. The *dharma* of Indian thought and the "natural law" of mediaeval European thought are at bottom systems of judgments of this kind. And since the main types of human relationship are constant, while the accidental circumstances in which they have to be worked out are open to change, we find quite naturally that there are variations within the main departments of moral teaching : for instance, the *dharma* concerning host and guest is different in a society where there are no inns from what it is in modern Britain, and the law concerning the suppliant in Homeric society bears obvious relations to the prevailing state of insecurity in those days.

It is interesting to distinguish and describe the main types of relationship and the types of conduct which we expect of one another in them. In itself this is a sociological question, but it is not without importance for ethics, because it seems as if different types of moral theory arise from taking one or other of the main types of relationship as the norm for all. We may distinguish, among others, three interesting types of relationship.

(1) Between *strangers* : I mean that relation which arises between people who meet casually on a single occasion, *e.g.* fellow-travellers in a train, or a shopkeeper and a strange customer, or a man who has lost his way and the passer-by whom he accosts. Here there is no necessary affinity of character between the parties, no permanent common purpose, no important degree of intimacy, but merely the accident of being thrown together on this one occasion. It is the thinnest relation possible between men ; yet even here the obligations of courtesy and helpfulness are generally recognised.

(2) Between *associates* : This is the relation set up by co-operation in fulfilment of a common purpose. Such common purposes can be of very various kinds and degrees of importance, and the associations resulting from them may be short-lived or long-lived and may make greater or lesser demands on the associates. In each case, however, their association rests not upon personal attraction or devotion, but upon the common purpose, and each associate has other interests and purposes which stand outside the scope of the association. When these conflict with the common purpose they act as disruptive forces, and the association has to defend itself against them by organisation, or at least by creating a public opinion and a spirit of loyalty. The association-relationship therefore involves a rough balance of interests between the associates, which is commonly called justice ; and this is the sphere in which that conception is especially at home.

(3) Between *fellows* : I give this name to the relationship based on an affinity felt by one person for another, which depends rather on what they both are than on particular assignable interests which they share. The affinity may be of various kinds, and may give rise to various relations extending through the different levels of friendship to the deepest levels of love and intimacy. When a relationship has to be organised or reduced to rule, it has sunk from a fellowship to a mere association. The governing principle of fellowship is love, in one of the senses of that very ambiguous word, and this is the peculiar sphere of love in human relationships. (It should be said, however, that the word " love " is used by some people, where Kant would say " respect ", to describe that mutual disponibility which underlies all the types of relationship, and of which the specific virtues are so many variants.)

This analysis leads me to a further conjecture as to what Professor Mackinnon means by those passages in which he emphasises the complexity of personal relationships and the difficulty (he says impossibility) of expressing them in terms of general formulæ. The Kantian ethic, with its emphasis on equality and no exceptions before the law, seems to be an excellent analysis of the distinctive nature of associate morality. It and other rigoristic theories of the same type go wrong, it seems, not in their analysis of associate morality itself, but in offering this as an account of morality *sans phrase*. They give no account of the distinctive nature of fellowship morality, and that is why they are often felt to be " cold " and inhuman. The existentialists, on the other hand, and personalists like Buber, represent historically a protest against the advance of collectivism and against collectivist social theories like those of Hegel and Marx. Their metaphysical and metapsychological speculations are to be seen as symptoms of an individuality driven to introspection and at the same time to an intensive cultivation of the most intimate human relationships, and it is therefore natural that they should have had something to tell us about that sphere of life which I have called fellowship. If there is any sphere of life which may seem to go easily into a formula, it is surely that of association with its governing principle, justice. If there is a sphere whose complexity defies analysis and whose very essence lies in delicate adjustments between unique individuals, it is surely that of fellowship. But if the disciple of Buber makes this a rule for the whole of moral theory, is he not as much out of balance in his own way as was Kant?

Now, what is it that underlies this interest in persons, whose manifestations are so various, but which seems in its unity and its diversity to be a main clue to the moral life? It depends on two factors, of which one is cognitive and the other is not so.

The cognitive factor is our understanding of one another. I use the word "understanding" here with the full meaning which has been given to it by Dilthey and his followers. I know what it is to be a man. I know it intimately, from within, because I am a man, and I not only have experiences like other men, but can reflect on them. I have some vague idea also of what it must be to be a horse, though in detail I cannot understand the horse with anything like the fulness or accuracy with which I understand a man like myself. I have no idea at all of what it is to be a stone; indeed, I am not sure that the question has any definite meaning. But the understanding which I have of human life like my own is not merely, as Dilthey maintains, the epistemological foundation of the *Geisteswissenschaften*; it is also the cognitive side of the foundation on which morality rests. It brings me into the presence of other human beings not merely as animals of the same species as myself, but as beings who have thoughts and feelings and purposes. These thoughts and feelings and purposes of theirs, so far as I become aware of them, awaken responses in me, and I know too that my own thoughts, feelings and purposes, so far as I give them expression, evoke responses in other people. On this foundation rests the possibility of all those relationships which are distinctively human.

But this alone does not suffice to determine the character

of these relationships. It is conceivable that I might understand other persons quite correctly and profoundly, and yet remain indifferent to what I know of them. This does not in fact normally happen; only a disease of mind or body, or an intolerable load of work or suffering, or a hard ascesis long practised, can bring me to a state of such indifference. Dilthey observes that understanding and appreciation, though logically distinguishable, are in real life inseparable. And the love or reverence for other persons, which animates my conduct so far as it is moral, is an appreciative attitude, made up of affective and volitional elements, and not a form of cognition. And therefore there is and can be, in my consciousness, no reason for it. It is one of those " passions " whose " slave " reason " is and ought only to be ". Nor can I give a reason to anyone else, to persuade him to adopt this attitude if he does not do so already. All I can do, in argument with one who denies my moral judgments, is to try to show him that he does in fact love his fellow men, and that in thinking he does not he is under an illusion.

Professor Mackinnon ends his paper with two questions which he says confront the present-day moralist. What can we now say to his two questions?

(1) " What exactly is it to be a person ? " This reads more like a metaphysical question than an ethical one, and we may perhaps feel inclined to rule it out of order in this context. Should he not rather ask " What is it that makes us take an interest in persons ? " The answer to this has just been given. It is our capacity for understanding, evoking our response of reverence or love. But this is something about us, the subjects who respect persons, not about the persons whom we respect. The answer is more psychological than metaphysical.

(2) " How does one authenticate the claim that one is inclined to make for characteristically personal existence ? " That is, I suppose, " how can we show that persons are important ? " Answer : We cannot, if " showing " means giving a reason over and above the fact that we are what we are and we love and reverence what we love

and reverence. Of course, it is conceivable that someone might give a metaphysical or a biological account of what *causes* us to respond in this way to our own kind, but that would not be a *reason* why we *should*.

There is, however, a third question which might be asked, a question of real practical importance, and it is this: "How can we prevent the sense of the importance of persons from being overlaid and stifled by other motives and interests?" The danger has always been there; for the moral consciousness has never been the sole system of motives operating in man. It is perhaps more serious today than it has been for some centuries on account of the pressures which social history is bringing to bear and the changes in our outlook which are in process of taking place. It is certain that the power-cult which stands at the centre of many modern movements is incompatible with the reverence for persons which has been Mackinnon's theme and mine. It is probable that the intellectual habits associated with scientific work are, if not incompatible with this reverence, at least inimical to it. These forces, relatively new in man's history, are in process of bringing about changes in his ways of thinking and living which we cannot see to their end. Those who do not wish to let morality as hitherto known go by default must ask themselves what forces they can put into the field against those which are making the drift. It seems unlikely that an answer will be found quickly and easily, if it is found at all.

III.—*By* JOHN WISDOM.

1. PROFESSOR MACKINNON is right it seems to me and on a matter of importance—those who write books on ethics seldom take ethical problems seriously. In his paper he gives hints as to what he means by this. He says that writers like Kierkegaard, Buber and Marcel are significant because they do take ethical problems seriously, while it is plain from what he says elsewhere that he would say that the utilitarians, for example, do not. It is plain too that he thinks that there is a connexion between not taking ethical problems seriously and, to use his own words, " trying resolutely to eliminate from the discussion any appeal whatsoever to that which transcends observation ".

2. There seems to me confusion over this last point. Sidgwick and Moore are utilitarians and don't take ethical problems seriously in MacKinnon's sense, yet both are transcendentalists who say that " good " is neither a word like " irritable " which tells us what a man is like nor a word like " irritating " which tells us how people feel to him. They say that goodness is a special kind of quality apprehended in a special way.

I would like to make two points here :—

(1) I am not saying that an anti-transcendental account of the role of ethical utterances doesn't make against " taking ethics seriously ". On the contrary such a meta-ethic when subjective may seem to make it impossible to take ethics seriously. And this can cause distress. About a year ago I was talking to a man who had been reading that ethical statements really express our feelings. Some philosophers have spoken as if we cannot show an ethical statement to be correct or find it incorrect. This sort of thing had led to or increased in this man a feeling of despair, a feeling that nothing really matters, a feeling that the world is water, without form and void. And this was not a man with a " half-baked " acquaintance with the meta ethics that affected him. I said to him, " Suppose the

goodness of a person were as objective as the goodness of an argument ". " Ah ", he said, " but is it ? "

A few weeks ago someone complained to me that so many people felt at a loss about values and asked whether there was'nt someone who gave help in that matter. Here again we come on ethical uneasiness, ethical distress, and upon the wish, the need, to make ethical effort.

To understand the despair which finds confirmation in subjectivism imagine a child who has been struggling to do what his mother and father want and suddenly notices that they are laughing at him.

One may say indeed that a subjective meta-ethics though it may temporarily smother the need for ethical effort may also by refusing to meet that need bring it into the open. One may say too that the idea that there are experts on living as there are experts on cooking is an illusion, and an illusion which cannot be cured without going through the feeling which subjectivism expresses, the feeling that there is no land and that therefore the sooner one stops swimming the better. Subjectivism makes one realise one must choose.

At the same time one may feel that the idea that there are experts on living as there are on cooking or the management of sheep is not an illusion—there are after all people with extra experience and insight into life.

(2) But I submit that it is not only subjective meta-ethics which in some ways makes it difficult to " do ethics seriously ". A transcendental meta-ethics may also have this effect. A subjective meta-ethics over emphasizes and in crude forms over simplifies the place of the sentiments in ethical effort. A transcendental meta-ethics, on the other hand, over-intellectualizes the process and sterilizes it. Professor Stebbing wrote a book called *Ideals and Illusions*. It is true that no one can say that this book encouraged one to take ethics easily. In it a great deal is said about getting clear about ideals and this is not represented as easy. But when I read the book I had the feeling that little or nothing was done in it to help one to get clear about ideals *except by indirection*. (By indirection something

was done, indeed it was. For the honesty and courage which appears between the lines even in so dry a work as Sidgwick's *Methods of Ethics* was also between the lines of *Ideals and Illusions*.) The very phrase " getting clear " takes one out of ethical distress into intellectual effort and *ipso facto* away from doing ethics seriously, since for that the intellect *by itself* is helpless.

When we wish to present the meaning, the function, the role of a class of sentences which perform a role complicated and peculiar compared with others we tend to do so by presenting them as being about an object or objects obscure to observation like a man behind the scenes or blocks of very transparent ice. We guess at the nature, condition and movements of an arch criminal by putting together the small but observable manoeuvres of his satellites. Only occasionally do we catch a glimpse of him slipping by in a dark limousine. When we wish to make a statement to which our observations of many individual things are relevant we put that statement in a form which suggests this model of the man in the shadows and speak of, for example, the average man, the plain man, the dog, and so on. When we wish to make statements to which many observations of two sorts of event going together are relevant we speak of there probably being *a connexion* between events of these sorts. When in logic we make a statement to which many observations as to the usage of words are relevant and in a peculiar manner, we again put the statements in a form which suggests illusive objects, though the objects are now said to be abstract and the connexions between them timeless. No wonder that when we are asked to describe the role of such classes of statements and their relation to what we mention in supporting or refuting them we are apt to say that the relation is that which holds in the model which their form and so much of our practise with them suggests.

In certain situations the inappropriateness of the model is forced on our attention, we throw it aside and in an effort to present the closeness of the connexion between the class of statements with which we are concerned and the observations on which we in fact rely in making them, we identify the statements with descriptions of the observations, that is represent them as related to the observations like statements about the average man to observations of individual men. In thus representing the statements as descriptions of the observations we over simplify their mode of connexion with the observations and usually we over simplify our account of the relevant observations. Should it seem that in our efforts to get down to earth we have caricatured the statements we started with then this is explained away by saying that the caricature only represents their meaning in so far as they are susceptible of rational justification. They may have in addition an exclamatory, hortatory, emotive, imaginative, function, but this is represented as irrelevant to their logical position. Thus is the oneness of logic preserved regardless of expense.

How a narrow idea about justification leads to a metephysical drive towards scepticism or transcendentalism or positivism, how these doctrines correct each other and are all both wrong and right, I shall not attempt to set out here. But I would like to offer two examples of the practical, non-metaphysical growth of a positivistic doctrine, of its non-metaphysical usefulness and of the way it over-simplifies.

Suppose a man notices a tendency amongst others to make claims about causal connexion from an armchair and to carry on disputes about such claims without that vigorous and laborious field observation they really demand. Suppose he then becomes a positivist and says " Whether one thing is causally connected with another is a matter of whether when one happens the other does ". This is an over simplification but it does put our effort in the right place. A transcendentalist will continue to deplore the over-simplification. The complexity and difficulty of causal investigation will appear in his account. It will appear in the distorted form of the transparency and illusiveness of the object, the relation, which he insists the claim is about. Still it will appear. And it will do no harm provided he doesn't really take any notice of his own talk about the possibility of a shorter way to knowledge of causal connexion.

The transcendentalist who says that logical and philosophical questions are questions about the inter-relations of timeless objects so obscures by an inappropriate model the procedure that settles them that only where they are easy can they be settled and where they are hard we are paralysed. The positivist who says that they are questions about words so misrepresents the procedure proper to them by an over simple model that however serious and difficult they are we can't take them seriously and carefully. Meta-metaphysics has had a powerful influence on metaphysics, i.e., description of the role of metaphysical sentences has had a powerful influence on the way we proceed with them. In contrast description of the role of sentences about material things has practically no effect on our firmly established procedure—metaphysics cuts no ice with train-starters. Meta-ethics has some influence on ethics. It is easy to exaggerate that influence and easy to underestimate it.

3. To return. MacKinnon wants ethical problems taken seriously, and perhaps we ought to say that he wants them taken seriously not merely by people who have a particular problem to deal with, but also by people who are dealing with a problem of some generality even though, as in a problem play, the problem is presented through a particular case.

Connected with this which is, I believe, his main concern are two other points : (1) He thinks that many ethical problems are better put in terms of people than in terms of acts. Thus he says that writers like Kierkegaard, Buber and Marcel raise the problem of the individual. He also says that Butler, as opposed to a utilitarian, argues that the proper subject of the moralist is the individual or person in his nature and in his relation with his fellows, and that he refuses consequently to allow that we can so to speak " absorb ethical reflection in discussion of the means of promoting good ".

(2) MacKinnon insists that the results of ethical reflection are not something that can be presented in a principle

or set of principles. He says that Butler and Kant are wrong if they suppose that ethical ideas can be conceived in terms of a general formula. " The use of any such formula ", he says, " can only have the effect of drawing an artificial boundary to contain that which in its nature cannot be contained. The responsiveness of man to man, the "disponability " of a man in the presence of his fellows, the diversity of human love—these are not things that can be mapped. You cannot set out even in the most rarified formula what is that which through the intimacies of personal exchange a man is called to become ".

4. But to consider these points. And first someone may ask " What is it to take ethical problems seriously ? Don't we all want to take them seriously ? Don't too many of us take them seriously ? Who doesn't take them seriously ? Hume, Bentham, Mill, Sidgwick, Moore or Ross ? " MacKinnon says : In utilitarianism one encounters a clear example, clear to the point of a caricature, of the approach to ethics which refuses altogether to take personal existence seriously. You see this in the insistence that the notion of happiness is fundamentally simple, that in effect happiness can be so defined as to constitute the twin of the whole analysis. It is insisted that in human satisfaction there is nothing mysterious ".

4.1. One may pick up a book on art and it be very dull. It is dull when it tries to give rules, canons, which will enable us to deduce whether a picture or a poem is good. It is dull when it tries to set out in general terms what makes a good picture good. Like a logician sets out what makes a good demonstration good. It happens that this can be done for demonstrations* with a very high degree of success. A

---

* And also for the statements of the form "p gives probability to q " where q is a specification of p, i.e. where q entails n. This is a very different class of statements from those of the same form of which it is true merely that p entails *It is probable that q*. The former are simply entailment statements about p and q reversed and in their case degrees of probability are obtained in so far as there are conventions about degrees of *specification* or *over-entailment*. Thus " A die lies with a six up " over-entails 1 to 6 " A die lies with either a one or a two or a three or a four or a five or a six up ". When p is about the past or present and q is not, but e.g. about the future the conditions for the goodness of argument from p to q cannot be satisfactorily set out in formulæ.

short statement of the necessary and sufficient conditions of formal perfection is presented in axioms and just what the axioms cover can be set out more and more specifically for anyone who wishes this done. Even here there is danger of the explanation being taken to be more adequate than it is. It can lead to shallowness and to blunting of the sense of the soundness of arguments in a ridiculous submission to the rules which should serve and co-operate with that sense.

When it comes to what makes a good picture good or a good poem good the whole plan is a failure and is apt to lead not to understanding and discriminating feeling for what is good, but to that rigid and dead reaction to recognised points sometimes found in dog fanciers and characteristic of the pharisees.

It is the same with a book on ethics which tries to set out what makes right acts right and good men good. Even if the author has given up as futile the idea of setting out conditions necessary and sufficient for goodness or rightness and merely tries to set out a list of the circumstances which are always, if present, considerations for or against an act, the game is a bore and a menace. For in this game he confines himself to the evident and thus to the obvious.

The only ethical principles worth attention are ones which are false like " Dishonesty to oneself is the only crime ". They do represent serious ethical effort when they are first hand.

(I think no one now pretends to give formulæ adequate for the moral life. To quote a few platitudes *as examples in order to illustrate the conflict of duties*—here I think of Ross—is quite a different matter though I am not sure that Ross said enough to make clear that he neither regarded the platitudes he quoted as interesting in themselves nor thought them capable of covering ethics.)

4.2. One may pick up a book on art and it not be dull.

To some people it will not be dull if it contains a lot of stories about painters, writers and musicians—how one was very poor and kept a little dog and so on. But that's not æsthetics.

To some people it will not be dull if it is about what beauty is, what sort of difference there is between two people when one praises a poem and the other says it's very poor. But that's meta-æsthetics.

There is however a third and proper way in which a book on art may not be dull. Mr. Lionello Venturi who writes the introduction to the Phaidon Botticelli helps one to see Botticelli. Mr. Edmund Wilson, the author of *Axel's Castle*, helps one to a juster apprehension of the works he writes about. In general a good critic by his art brings out features of the art he writes about, or better, brings home the character of what he writes about, in such a way that one can feel and see, see and feel that character much better than one did before. Such a critic tackles æsthetic problems, with his head and with his heart, with his heart and with his head and so tackles them seriously.

It is worth noticing how such revealing, moving talk, such rhetoric, as his, need not be directed towards showing that a work is good or bad. It may be directed simply towards showing it to us for what it is. It may be directed for example to showing us that though Mr. Thornton Wilder's *Heaven's my Destination* and much of the work of Mr. Thurber at first seem comic, they are really tragic. Chekov called *The Cherry Orchard* a comedy. But obviously anyone perfectly content with this description has not, as we say, understood *The Cherry Orchard*. Mr. Venturi writes, p. 13, of the Introduction to the Phaidon Botticelli, " In the episodes from the life of St. Zenobius we find a new chromatic tendency. Not only do all the individual colours assume a new intensity but their relationship with one another is based entirely on contrasts and oppositions. This does not result in a bursting forth of light for the contrast is not one of complementary colours functioning as light and shadow. It is a contrast of tints, expressing dramatic despair with its own means."

The art of giving us a fuller apprehension of a work of

P

art is a wider æsthetics, a wider activity than that of showing that it is beautful or ugly.

Primary art itself, very often, reveals the familiar, shows us what we have looked at but not seen. A poem may show us swans as birds which survive from a world of colour and light before the sad, dim morning of the Fall or again as swans on a river, as it might be three ducks on a pond. Our eyesight may be all right or at least good enough to enable us to see a bandstand in a Park. And yet a picture of the bandstand in the park may make us say " I never noticed how here the bizarre meets the banal and dread hunts gaiety up spiral pillars to the sky." In short an artist may enable us to see what we have looked at so often and never seen or even to see again what we had lost the power to see. After writing this I opened Oscar Wilde's *The Decay of Lying* and read "To look at a thing is very different from seeing a thing. One does not see anything until one sees its beauty. . . . At present, people see fogs, not because there are fogs, but because poets and painters have taught them the mysterious loveliness of such effects." He ought to have said surely that one does not see a thing until one sees its ugliness, its charm, its grace, its banality, and so on. Mr. Rylands in his introduction to his Shakespeare anthology, *The Ages of Man*, says that Samuel Johnson decided that Shakespeare's plays are not tragedies or comedies but "compositions of a distinct kind exhibiting the real state of sublimary nature which partakes of good and evil, joy and sorrow, mingled with endless variety of proportion and innumerable modes of combination."

5. And of course it is possible to do ethics seriously. Novelists do often. *Crime and Punishment*, *Anna Karenina*, *The Brothers Karamazov*, Mr. Marquand's *G. H. Pulham Esq.*, Mr. Green's *The Heart of the Matter*, Mr. de la Mare's *The Almond Tree*, are all novels in which this is done. Something particular is presented, but so presented that in it something universal is seen through without any attempt to net in a formula the infinite idiosyncracy of the stuff of Time. A critic speaks perhaps of a particular picture and

just that picture is his subject. But somehow he so speaks that we can the better see not only that picture but others also. When Rembrandt paints an old woman's head just that old woman's head is what he paints. At the same time we want to say that it is by no means just that old woman's head that he has painted.

It is possible to make in ethics and æsthetics remarks which are general and still not worthless. This happens when some value is temporally undervalued or perhaps has always been undervalued. Clive Bell emphasized the importance of the formal features of a work of art by saying that beauty depends entirely upon these. Nietsche re-emphasized certain values apt to be underestimated in Christian ethics. And Christ emphasized certain values which perhaps had never been adequately emphasized. The phrase to emphasize a neglected value stands for a process which can be small and can be big enough to demand a very big man.

The novels which I have mentioned could be called studies of acts, but clearly they are better called studies of persons. A person is an exceedingly complex pattern in time. Anything which helps us to see the pattern in the apparently largely chaotic procession of incidents which make up a person's life story helps us to " see him for what he is," just as remarks which order the incidents of a novel for us help us to see that novel for what it is and remarks which order the parts of a visual or auditory pattern help us to see or hear that pattern for what it is. There are general psychological remarks which can very much help us in making sense out of nonsense just as other scientific hypotheses have made sense out of a chaos of facts.

I would like to add that I am aware that the novels I spoke of are not primarily ethical studies in the ordinary sense of studies with a view to a verdict " Good " or " Bad." In a court of law, even when the facts are agreed upon, the situation is studied with a view to a verdict, but the verdict is expressed not in critical words like " good " and " bad " but in words like " murder in the first degree ", " manslaughter ", " negligence ", and so on. The novels I mentioned are special efforts to see people for what they are. This is not an exotic process but one which in some degree goes on in us all the time we are concerned with others.

How understanding of people is connected with ethics I shall not here try to say. But this much may be said : before we pay much attention to a man's judgment of others, whether ethical or not, we must have confidence that he understands them and that we understand him so that we may understand his judgment of them.

6. Wider æsthetics and wider ethics are, I realize, not metaphysics or philosophy in the sense in which I have been using these words, but they are, I submit, connected with metaphysics in two ways worth mentioning. First it is part of the business of metaphysics to eorrect misleading accounts of what they are in the same way that it corrects misleading accounts of any other procedure for discovery, such as mathematics and metaphysics. And this is necessary although we have been familiar with the æsthetic and ethical procedures for centuries.

Second there is a likeness between the techniques used in art criticism, ethics, and art on the one hand and metaphysics on the other. Selection of the typical, caricature. metaphor, paradox, all are used to discover the familiar.

Suppose we call all such attempts to see things for what they are, to find the reality in appearance, philosophy or metaphysics. Then we begin to understand why people who are not philosophers obstinately expect something of philosophy of which they feel cheated if we tell them that philosophy is the curing of mental cramp which has been induced by the fascination of certain analogies suggested by our language, by too narrow an idea of the logic of our language. They still feel cheated when we offer the more positive description that philosophy is the meta-study which attempts to gain a better grasp of the notes of categories of sentences.

There are in people two feelings here : (1) that philosophy is wider than the study of how we know the categories matter, mind, time, space, necessity, value, (2) that even this study of the categories is not adequately described as a certain sort of study of words.

I believe there is a good deal of illusion and confusion here. Light is thrown on our desire to bring philosophy nearer to life in J. O. Wisdom's study " Three Dreams of Descartes " in *The International Journal of Psychoanalysis*, Vol. XXVII, Part I, and less directly in his study of Schopenhauer. At the same time metaphysics can come into literature. For example there are one or two places in Proust where it can be seen how metaphysics can grow out of life and how metaphysics can help us to show ourselves life. After I had written this sentence I happened to open a collection of essays by the Greek poet Demetrios Capetanakis and there read " There are moments in Proust's work when the need to find a solution in philosophy of the most urgent problems of existence is so painful that we begin to feel that we cannot go on. We summon our intelligence to our aid, to give us a moment of rest, of respite ; but only a moment, because philosophic anxiety can never cease. . . . Proust's affirmation, for instance, that love is only a kind of madness and that the individuality of the person we love is an illusion, has nothing definitive about it. We turn the page, and we find Proust fighting with all his strength to find another solution to this problem that in reality has no solution."

Those who think that philosophy can help are apt to think that philosophers have some special knowledge which enables them to answer the questions that trouble the enquirer or that he has a technique which the enquirer himself has not which if applied to the questions of life might solve them. What the philosopher in the narrower sense of one who studies the procedures suitable to various categories of question can do is to make clearer what procedure is suitable to these questions about what this and that really is. It then appears that the suitable procedure is like his own when he asks what value, necessity, mind and matter really are.

We may now recall that such statements as " There are

no acts which are really unselfish ", " There are no acts which are really free" and even such typical metaphysical paradoxes as " No one really knows what goes on in the mind of another ", " There is really no such thing as matter ", " Nothing is really good or bad, it is only that we regret some things and not others ", are not themselves meta-statements, that is they are not statements about statements. They are statements which in the ordinary usage of language are false, they are statements in a new language which is a distortion of ordinary language. One way of answering " What point have these paradoxes? " is to reply " They show up the roles, the inter-relations between the roles, of categories of statements (or sentences) ", but another way of answering is to reply " They show up the nature of, the inter-relations between categories of rational procedure, of thought ", and another way of answering is to reply " They show up the nature of the inter-relations between categories of fact, of being ". And with this we return to the starting point of our circular tour through " Philosophy is about words ".

When someone, Proust perhaps, says " Individuality is an illusion " or " Love is madness " it is something about the world which he has grasped and felt which forces him to make these outrageous statements. " Altruism is an illusion ", " Value is an illusion ", " Mind is an illusion ", " The rationality of scientific reasoning is an illusion " arise in a way which though it is different and more a matter of confusion about words is yet not altogether different.*

I have represented all these paradoxes as coming wholly from reflection on things already experienced, but " Individuality is an illusion ", " Love is an illusion ", "Altruism is an illusion," may, as we know, come in part from new experience—surprises, disappointments. " The table isn't solid ", " The sun we see is the sun which existed 8 minutes ago ", " Every sound is everywhere ", " People have thoughts and feelings they don't know of ", come

---

* John Wisdom, *Other Minds*, Supp. vol. xx.

largely or in part from discovery of new facts. Scientists, as we know, are not all or only concerned with collecting new facts. What is more they are not concerned only with predicting the future. Copernicus gave us a new picture of the world. Freud makes sense out of nonsense. Science of this kind, philosophy and certain art are akin in that they reveal what lies not behind or beyond but hidden in the obvious.